THE COST OF FREEDOM

RAFAEL FELLOVÉ

El costo de la libertad
FL
CUBA

The Cost of Freedom
Rafael Fellové

Published by *Spines*
ISBN: 979-8-89569-377-3

CONTENTS

PROLOGUE

This book you hold in your hands today contains a life lesson. There are times when you have to pay a very high price to obtain something.

The life of every man becomes like a magical tale written by the hand of God.

Some of us always live under a sky that portends a storm, and others know how to discover the shine of the stars, even through the darkest clouds. Today, after some years have passed, it is interesting for me to understand and learn how our attitudes change as we mature with age. Each stage of life brings new needs, beliefs, questions, and answers. Today we can look back at what once was with some gratitude. Because it has brought us to where we are now, alive and healthy.

I feel deeply moved and influenced, (identified) with this story of "THE COST OF FREEDOM" and I also feel honored and privileged that RAFAEL FELLOVE OLVERA asked me to write a brief Prologue for this book.

This is a work that leads the reader to delve into the story of those who have been relegated from their parents, relatives, friends, and their homeland to seek freedom. A small word of eight letters, but one that holds great satisfaction and happiness when you obtain it.

According to my dictionary, "FREEDOM" means: Absence of obligation. The state of a nation that is NOT dominated by a tyrannical power. The state of a person who is not a prisoner or who does not depend on anyone. The power to do what is not forbidden, to act at will, the ability to act as we want without any obligation, a way of speaking, freedom of movement.

Proposing to continue in friendship with life as a celebration of human quality, still possessed despite everything. Learned that not everything has to be their way, that the world does not end when we are rejected and abandoned. Pain and emptiness are felt, but they are part of life, not its end.

He never hid behind bitterness, fear, or apathy. Instead, he discovered his inner freedom and continues standing firm, free from restraints; facing any challenge that prevents him from seeing life with optimism; rising from the bottom.

His spirit and positive attitude have allowed him to pull and boost his life from the abyss and emerge towards a new life, standing tall so that life does not tear him apart; focused on the present, never hesitating to start something new, if convinced it is the right thing to do.

His evolution has involved continually improving in every aspect of his being and finally, over time, obtaining the best outcomes. He cannot change the past. But today, beginning with the end in mind makes it possible for his life to have a purpose and a promising future.

There will always be an ideal moment to start improving oneself, and it is NOW.

There are situations in the world that cause us admiration, one of them being a human being who knows how to endure misfortune with courage. Magic and miracles happen only to people who are willing to do something for themselves; let's say you can make any dream come true if you cling to it tenaciously, ask God for help with faith, and never give up. Whatever your cross, whatever your pain, the sun will always rise after the rain.

My finite mind cannot comprehend why so much hatred, so much greed, and the disease of power of a Communist Government and Ideal are selfish, not caring how to bring a good end to the destiny of a people in need.

Many decades have passed, and still, the voices clamoring for Freedom remain active, and the echo still resonates for those who lost their lives in the attempt to seek their freedom.

It is difficult to live in a country under the shadow of Communism, where human rights do not count but are rather violated; a gag law exists, where there is no freedom of expression; you can think freely but not act. The only freedom one has is what the Government authorizes, a conditioned freedom. After living a miserable childhood full of shortages and a youth of forced labor, with bad treatments, beatings, humiliations, and insults, and having experienced the impunity and deceit of authorities and the betrayal of a Communist Government.

Rolando Castillo took the courage to meet a new possibility of freedom, drawing strength from the depths of his soul to be able to renounce his family and leave in search of a better future.

The desire to breathe the pure air of freedom kept him standing amidst so much misfortune, and when he thought he had achieved it, he once again faced adversity. With new challenges and obstacles in a country with another language.

Other customs, different laws with a system disguised as freedom, where the real business is imprisonment.

The weight of Pain could be seen through his eyes. Loneliness, sadness, and depression invaded the feeling, causing nostalgia. Coupled with all that, it made him weep, stifled within himself.

He thought the world had collapsed on him because things - did not turn out the way he expected.

Having a life of captivity against his will, sailing in an ocean of problems and without a defined course, Rolando fought against everything that came his way. But within his heart, he knew there was a small light of hope at the end of the tunnel, that not everything could be dark in his life.

Rolando Castillo had incredible inner strength, he brought out the grit and potential to fight with life itself.

His elevated mood was affected by adversity and I think no one is exempt from a situation like that, but he never took a negative or pessimistic attitude; on the contrary, he took courage and responsibility to correct any mistakes and thus be able to amend his personal life.

INTRODUCTION

I have written this book with the aim of making known the suffering that exists with the communist regime in Cuba for those of us who do not agree with it. As a result of that political system imposed in my country, there has been a series of escapes from decades ago until now. I wrote particularly about one that took place in the 1980s. It was one of the largest in the history of Cuba and known as "The Mariel Boatlift". However, in this book, and as a personal story, I want to point out that many people were expelled for being homosexuals, criminals, disabled, mentally ill, or simply for being anti-communists.

In my case, I always looked for a way to leave my country until one day an opportunity presented itself and I took it, tired of the depressing economic situation in which the Cuban people live. I remember that, at that time, we left those of us protected by the Peruvian Embassy, just like others who, as I said before, were expelled against their will by Fidel Castro.

It is difficult to live in a country where children do not have a childhood; however, they acquire responsibilities at such an early age. At seven or eight years old, I noticed that we did not have enough to eat at home. So, I decided to help my mother so that we would not suffer so much hunger.

In Cuba, many children of that age begin to mature by facing problems that are typical of adults. Our childhood is truncated due to the needs that are so evident in our homes.

Perhaps with the story I present in this book, you will learn about the pain, frustration, courage, and sadness that many of us Cubans feel when we see that shackles have been placed on our hands and feet, as well as gags in our mouths to neither say nor do anything before a regime we have been forced to accept. Those of us who disagree are imprisoned or killed.

In the year 1980, when I left Cuba, the situation was too difficult because, just like now, we had nothing to eat. If anything, we were given a very limited monthly ration of rice, beans, oil, and other basic foods, which were not enough for the month. Due to these problems, we are forced to escape in search of a better future, leaving behind our family and all the loved ones.

I never imagined that after achieving such long-awaited freedom, I would have to face other problems. "To achieve what one desires, it costs a lot, and the price must be paid." I have always remembered the words my mother told me days before I left my beloved Cuba. In my case, I have had to avoid loneliness in one way or another to move forward. I have had to hide my feelings of pain, which I will show until the day I can see my mother and siblings.

Eighteen years without seeing them, but I have the hope of one day embracing them, then my heart will be relieved a little. Like me, there are more Cubans who have suffered and are suffering;

for that and much more, these words have come from within my soul.

I decided to write this book because my wife motivated me to do it; after telling her my experiences and making my resentment and pain known, she suggested that if I expressed these feelings, my emotional situation would change, and I would then see things differently.

I would have liked to arrive in this country in the company of my family. I missed the advice and support of my mother and siblings. In my case, I was alone and I didn't care what happened to me. In reality, loneliness led me to underestimate myself and to decide hastily regarding my feelings, all in the desire to have someone to trust and share my life with. Unfortunately, I made such mistakes that I paid dearly for them.

I remember that when I left the shelter in Indian Village, I looked at the street, the houses, and the people in a different way. Maybe because everything was prettier than in my country, I thought everything was more pleasant. However, over the years, I have realized that human values have been lost.

Personally, I was dazzled by the ease with which money is obtained through dirty dealings. So I got into the business of buying and selling drugs, and I started drinking beer and smoking marijuana. I got involved with women who were in my same environment. And I always behaved well with them. I didn’t have enough experience when it came to women; I believed that with one of them I would manage to form a family. Since, like many Cubans who are alone in this country, I also wished to have a home. I currently have it and will never let it slip away.

At that time, the blows I received from life were so many that I noticed how my character was changing little by little. I became irritable, always on the lookout to respond to any aggression. After all, I did not lose my human values. Despite all the betrayals that people did to me, I always gave them the best of myself. And I know I acted wrongly, but I also know that I have the satisfaction of not having caused harm to those around me.

Later, I was forced to live in a world where everything is harsher... in jail. There, my life, which was already hurt, was further shattered. Then, in that place, loneliness, sadness, depression, and other feelings that make a person feel powerless, insecure, etc., took hold of me even more, leading some people to suicide on several occasions.

When I went to jail, I wasn't charged with drug offenses, but I stayed there for three years without being told the reasons for my confinement. During that time, I always thought that it was a mistake to come to this country and that perhaps it would have been better to stay in Cuba, even with the regime that keeps my country dead alive. In prison, I wrote several love letters, since that feeling is what prisoners lack the most. I understand that when someone goes to prison it's because they committed a crime, and depending on the severity, the person is judged and sentenced. But there are also people who, like me, don't know why they are there and have been shouting that they are innocent. Now that I am free, I think of all the Cubans who are still imprisoned because when Mr. Fidel Castro forcibly removed them from Cuba, he said they were the worst criminals. When in fact, many of them were innocent.

Despite everything, I always had in mind a phrase that helped me a lot to survive at that time and to keep doing so.

"Do not let past mistakes
prevent you from seeing future opportunities."

1
ROLANDO, THE CHILD

When I think of my beloved Cuba, I feel an irresistible nostalgia. I remember its beautiful typical streets, its brick houses with cement roofs, its blue sky, the gentle and rhythmic sea breeze, the bright and hot sun, the fresh air that, when passing by, makes the palm trees sway, mango trees, guava trees, and the plants lying on the ground.

My street, in particular, was sloped and downhill; a river crossed it with a bridge by which the street continued uphill. At the end, the street was flat and connected to an orchard that belonged to the government. There were mango, mamey, avocado, orange, guava trees, ceiba palms, among others. What I liked most about that place was a well of crystal-clear water formed by the river among three palms, which is why we called it "The Three Palms". I remember we used to bathe there. There was also a very large dam, surrounded by tall and lush trees, palms, wild grass, and very soft green grass. My friends and I used to go fishing there.More than for fun, I went for fish to sell and help my mom, since the money my father sent was not enough for anything. At that time, sixty Cuban pesos was little money to maintain two boys and six girls. We were eight siblings, of which my sister Margarita, the oldest of all, was born with a problem in her feet; and for twelve years she was admitted to the Carlitos Garcías hospital. My mom Irma was with her every afternoon. The life we had was not easy. My mother also played the role of father and worked very hard to support us. I think that's why I was born with a tremendous desire to fight, just like my mother.

My house was small. In front was the porch, to the left there was a house very close to mine. On the right side, there was a garden with many flowers that my dad planted. Next to the garden was a hallway that connected to the backyard. Upon entering, there was the living room, followed by a bedroom and then the kitchen, which incidentally had a door to the garden. Next was the bathroom and finally, another room where my brother and I slept.

I remember that when my mom had to go with my sister to the hospital, she left us under the care of her friend Bertha. At that time, I worked delivering bread. When I finished my work, the bakery owners gave me rice, beans, bread, etc., and I took them home to help my family. I think Bertha didn't like that because, when arriving home, she cursed and humiliated me.

One day, when the Castro government cut the power for a couple of hours at night, my mom had to go to the hospital.

"Look, son," my mother said, "I'm going to the hospital to see your sister. Bertha will take care of you... but she's not here and I'm running late! Look, son, I'm going to leave you watching over your sisters and brother until she comes. Remember that today they will also cut the power!"

"Yes, mom, don't worry about that."

My mom left calmly and I, at seven years old, stayed to take care of my siblings. Minutes later, someone knocked on the door.

"Who's knocking on the door?" I asked.

"It's me!" shouted Bertha.

Then I opened and saw her massive shadow filtering through the doorframe. She was fat and tall. She finally came in.

"Ronaldito! Are the lanterns ready?" she asked me.

"Yes, Bertha, I prepared them myself," I replied fearfully. "I filled them with bright light for when the power goes out."

She didn't say anything and went to cool off in the backyard. Half an hour later, the power went out and Bertha returned inside the house.

"Ronaldito, come here! Fetch the lantern and give it to me!"

Somewhat afraid of her and the darkness we were in, I didn't dare go where she was, because she always mistreated me.

"The lantern is in the kitchen!" I replied. "Next to the bright light and the alcohol. Where the pots are."

Since I didn't go, Bertha got upset, as if I had said or done something wrong to her.

"Come on! Come on, little sissy, learn to be a man!" she said, giving me a shove. "Come on! So you can show me where the lantern is!"

Fearfully, I walked to the kitchen. I arrived and sat on the floor with my legs crossed. I searched for what she asked for so she wouldn't say anything more. In my hurry, I dropped a bottle of alcohol.

"Bertha!" I said to her, "Don't light any matches! Because I dropped the alcohol and don't know where it ran to! It might run toward the garden door!"

"Okay! Okay! I heard you already!" she said with an annoyed tone. "I'm not going to light any matches!"

Confident, I bent down again thinking she wouldn't light any matches. Suddenly, I saw a small light on the wet floor. Then I turned to look at her and she was lighting a cigarette. I continued searching for the lantern and found it. I lifted my face and looked at Bertha. I extended my hand to give it to her. She didn't take it because at that moment she threw the match with which she lit her cigarette onto the floor. The alcohol immediately ignited and the flames embraced my legs, for they were soaked in alcohol. I started shouting.

"Bertha! Help me! I'm burning!"

"What are you saying, boy?"

"I'm burning!" I repeated in desperation.

She stood still and then turned to see me. Then she saw I was telling the truth.

"Wait!" she said stupidly. "I'll get a blanket!"

I tried to extinguish my burning legs by rolling on the ground several times without success. When she returned, my legs were completely burned. She wrapped my legs in the blanket to extinguish them.

"Get up," she said with tremendous ignorance, "to see what happened!"

"But... I can't get up! I can't feel my legs! Look... take the lantern."

He grabbed the gossip and left it on the table. He ran to get help. Fortunately, some neighbors were in their doorway, and she told them what was happening to me. One of them, who had known me since I was a child, got up and came to see me.

“What's wrong with my little black one?” asked Margaro.

Upon seeing me quickly, he wrapped me in the comforter and took me up to his car. He took me to the same hospital where my sister was. Margaro had to say he was my father so that they would attend to me urgently. Immediately some doctors arrived and saw me so bad that they quickly moved me to a room. Two nurses arrived and held me by my feet and hands. A nurse came in, hands full of cold soapy water in basins. She cut my pants and began to remove the burnt areas with a bone brush. I screamed in pain and fainted. When I came to, the pain was even more intense. I looked toward a window beside me and saw Margaro watching me.

“Margaro!” I shouted, “My...”

I fainted again. I don't know how much time passed. The pain brought me back to consciousness again. I looked to see if Margaro was still at that window, but he was no longer there. I screamed and knew nothing more.

When I woke up, I saw a white light on the ceiling, which was painted the same color.

“Where am I?” I asked myself confusedly. I looked down and saw that my legs were bandaged and elevated. It seemed like they were going to experiment on me. I wanted to see my mother.

“What would Bertha have told my mom about all this?” I never knew.

On the other side of the window that separated our room from the hallway, I saw some people peeking in to see us, as if looking for someone. I realized it was visiting hour, and I started to look for my mother. Minutes later, I saw her arrive. I noticed a deep sadness in her eyes. Then she cried, and I felt my heart break. I wanted to run to kiss her and hug her, to tell her I was okay, not to cry anymore. She couldn't enter the room because it was prohibited as they could infect us with a virus. She always trusted me, and I know it hurt her to see me there like that.

The day of the Three Wise Men arrived, and I was about to turn a year in the hospital. My dear mother brought me a fire truck. I remember taking great care of it, as it was the only gift I had ever received in my life.

One night I felt cold. Next to my bed was a blanket, and I tried to grab it, but I fell to the floor and couldn't get up anymore. I tried to ask for help, but no one saw or heard me. I suppose the nurse on duty passed by and seeing the empty bed thought no one was in it. After waiting a long time for help, I fell asleep. The next morning, the morning shift nurse saw me and helped me up. I think she liked me very much.

"So you won't suffer," the nurse said kindly, "I'll leave you covered before I leave." From that day on, things changed; I no longer felt so alone. The nurse would visit me in the afternoons after her shift. She told me stories and spoke to me about interesting things. She grew fond of me, and I grew fond of her. She treated me like a son.

The doctor transferred me to the massage room, and I stopped seeing her. In that place, visitors could come in. Finally, I could have my mom near, and I hugged and kissed her. That was the happiest day of my life. My mother came every day. She stayed with me for a long time. The only thing that made me suffer were the massages, which initially were very painful. Later I felt them less.

"Madam, it's been four months that Ronaldito has been in the massage room," the doctor told my mom. "I'm going to discharge him, but before you leave, I want to talk to you."

"Yes, doctor, I'll go to your office before we leave," my mother replied. "Excuse me, when will you discharge him?"

"In two more days," the doctor affirmed. He opened the door and invited us into his office. "Take a seat, madam. I asked you to come because I want to tell you that you have a little man by your side, and he deserves to be healed. If I had the necessary resources, I would send him to another country for plastic surgery. Look," he paused, "as he grows, and people see his legs, he will be ashamed. Imagine when he has a girlfriend and they go to the beach, I don't think she'll like his legs."

Now that I think about it, what poor ethics that doctor had, how he scared me!

2

THE RECRUIT

Two and a half years later, I was still studying and in the afternoons working with some gentlemen who paid me twenty-five Cuban pesos every day. They also gave me rice, beans, bread, etc., but always in secret. One day, my father spoke with my mother and mentioned that he was going to get us some study scholarships so we could be something in life.

Six months later, my father gave us the scholarship, and I began studying at a Textile Engineering Technical School.

In 1974, I was expelled from school. Since there were quite a few pretty girls, I started to neglect my studies. I had problems with my classmates and several fights, which contributed to my departure from that School Center.

My mother didn't want me to leave school, so she got me a place in a workshop school, where I could study and continue working.

Sometimes I would meet with Reynaldo and Mayito to go fishing at the dam, the beach, or along the Malecón. Whenever we were there, we thought about getting into an Embassy or inventing something else to go to another country. That way I could fix my feet.

Reynaldo, Mayito, and I one day went fishing at the Morro of Havana. It's a place where there's a rocky promontory and the water is crystal clear. We were sitting and quiet, waiting for some fish to bite the hook.

"What do you think about starting to make a small boat to escape from Cuba?" I said, breaking the silence. "You see there's no future in this country. We're always going to be stuck here!"

"Don't be stupid, Ronaldito," Rey replied. "If we do it, we wouldn't even make it to the Gulf of Mexico before getting caught!"

I laughed resignedly and didn't comment again. The afternoon was already saying goodbye. The sky had an orange tinge with yellow; a few clouds adorned the sky. We got ready to leave. That day we didn't catch anything.

In my country, when boys turn fifteen, they must enroll in the military by law. Those who don't inform the military that they are of age to enlist, the military goes to their homes and puts them in jail. I was fifteen and decided to enroll. They told me they would send me a letter informing me of the day I had to show up to take a test, which, upon passing, signified that by turning sixteen, I would have to be with them for three years to fulfill the Mandatory Military Service.

My mother started working as the head of a kitchen that belonged to the government. She, along with four other women, cooked for two thousand five hundred people. Sometimes, my mother would wake me up early to go to her work and give me rice, beans, meat, bread, etc. I would take all those things home, and my sisters would cook them.

One day, mom didn't take me to her work. She was going to give me a pair of small chickens, two pounds of black beans, and some rice for my sister Margarita to cook before she came back from work. I left that kitchen and walked down the empty street heading to the bus stop. I arrived and leaned against a wall. I was very calm waiting for my bus. The morning was cool. The sun hadn't risen yet, and the sky was blue. There were no clouds. The ceiba palms up there swayed rhythmically. I lowered my gaze and saw a police car approaching. It was coming very slowly. When it arrived, the officers were looking at me, but I ignored them.

"Where are you coming from, kid?" they asked me.

"From my aunt's house," I replied very seriously.

"You're coming from your aunt's house so early?" they said with a tone of intrigue and at the same time amused, so I wouldn't be afraid of them.

I really hated them because they were abusers.

"Yes, I'm coming early because I have to study and want to go home first to drop this off. I'm also going for my books."

"And what's in that bag, kid?"

"It's something my aunt gave me for my mom."

"Come closer, kid. We want to check what's in that bag."

"And what did I do for you to mess with me?"

The officers ignored me. They got out of the car and took the bag from me. When they saw the chickens, rice, and beans, their expressions changed. They became very serious.

"You have to come with us," they said. "Show us your ID card!"

"Why do I have to go with you?"

"Show us your ID card!"

"I don't have my ID with me. I got to my aunt's house last night to sleep there. She is sick, and the food I'm carrying is for my mom to make some soup for her."

They didn't believe me and took me to the police station. They locked me up all day in a cell. My mom didn't know anything about me. She trusted that I was working. Meanwhile, at the police station, the officers kept questioning me.

"Look, kid, just tell us what you were doing at that time and with that bag of food."

"I already told you that I came from my aunt's house. She gave me this food for my mom to make some soup."

"No, we don't believe you. Better tell us where you stole it from!"

"I haven't stolen anything! Really!"

"Yes, you stole it!" they said. "Tell us from where!"

"Alright, alright. Fine! Where do your mom and dad work? What is your family like?"

"My dad works as a judge, and my mom in a kitchen. My family is the Castillo González."

When I gave them my dad's workplace address and my mom's, they immediately called. It was my father who showed up.

"It's good that you came, sir," they said to him. "Because your son was at the bus stop very early this morning with this bag of food. You know, this gives a different impression. We believe that he rather stole it."

"I don't think my son did that," he answered them.

"Well, his behavior is a bit suspicious. Look, your son says his aunt gave him the food, for your wife to make him a little soup. He also says you're a judge... I don't doubt that. But is it true?"

"Look, officer, the boy is telling the truth. I'm sure of it. Here, here is my ID. I work for the government."

"Mmh... true! Let me see. Oh! Sorry! I believe your son is telling the truth."

"See. I trust my son!"

"Come, come, Mr. Judge. Your son is in a cell. You know it's... a matter of security."

They immediately released me, apologizing for keeping me there for so long.

"Boy! Get out of there. You're free, we have cleared up the problem. You were right. Accept our apologies."

After that day, every time the police officers who stopped me saw me, they greeted me very smilingly and with great respect. My mom at that time had a boyfriend who always talked to me about the United States. I started to develop an interest in knowing another country. I wanted to heal my feet. Additionally, I wanted to have money to help my mom.

Six months after that, the military called me to present myself and undergo an exam, which I passed satisfactorily. I, having one more year, and those who needed three years because of school, who were already from the State, thought.

In that camp, we stayed for six months. Then we were transferred to a camp in a small village where there were also few houses, but the people there were happier and more friendly.

Our class schedule was from eight in the morning to twelve at noon; after class, we were given an hour to eat. And from one o'clock, they took us to a school that was being built. Each of us did the work corresponding to the career we were studying. The schools we were building had dormitories and were intended for those students who finished one school level and moved to another, for example, students who finished primary school and continued with secondary school, or students who finished high school and pursued a career. The government said that those students had to go to field schools like the one we were building, during the forty-five days of vacation given. Once settled in those study centers, they were given introductory and orientation courses about the next level they were going to study. They were given an hour for lunch. And then they went to work in the harvest of oranges, guavas, limes, etc., that were planted on government farms.

In the camp, I got along well with my companions. They always looked for me to work or to do mischief and tricks. In the small village, sugar cane was also planted. There were more trees and plants. I liked going with the companions on horseback. We went to the schools to joke with the girls, and we even had girlfriends.

"Ronaldito! I want you to help me. Look, this weekend I don't want to be on duty because I have a date with my girlfriend, and I don't want to miss it!" a worried recruit companion said to me. "I don't know what to invent. Nothing comes to mind."

"Well, Alberto, I have an idea," I said, smiling. "Unless the Sergeant gets tough and doesn't believe you're sick."

"Tell me what idea you came up with!" he replied with curiosity. "Because you're always inventing something."

"Listen to me well, and we'll go there," I said in a lower voice. "We grab a piece of iron from the railroad track. There, as it's always deserted."

"Go on! Go on, Ronaldito!"

"As I was saying, when we get there, you put your foot on the track, and I give you a slam, and your foot is sure to swell. When the Sergeant sees you, he'll want to give you a few days off."

"Yes! Yes! That's a good idea."

"You tell me when we do it," I asked.

"Today is Thursday. What do you think about tomorrow?"

"As you wish. Remember, there are only two days left for your guard duty," I commented.

"Near the dormitories, I found a one-inch pipe. It occurred to me to fill it with cement and let it dry. That day was hotter than usual, the cement dried quickly. The next day, Alberto insisted that we go to the railroad track."

"Ronaldito, let's go to the railroad track. Right now!" he insisted. "Better tomorrow," I answered.

"No! Let's go today!"

"Okay. Let's go to the track."

I took the pipe, but I didn't tell him it was filled with cement inside.

"Well, we are here, so now what?" he said to me.

"Now, put your foot on the train line but tilt it. Turn your face so you don't see when it hits you." I was prepared, and as soon as he turned his face, I hit him hard. He almost fainted.

"Oh! It hurts! Oh!"

He fell, tried to get up, but couldn't. I approached to see how his foot was. He rolled up his pants, and I saw the bone broken and sticking out from the side of his calf. I felt very bad. I thought I hadn't hit him that hard, but the facts spoke for themselves.

"Ronaldito? It wasn't that bad. Oh! It was just a soft hit. Oh! to make it swell. Oh! It hurt."

"I felt I didn't hit you that hard. Forgive me. I'm sorry. I helped him and took him to the camp. We had to tell them his foot got stuck on the track and suddenly a train appeared, and Alberto, out of desperation, pulled his foot out very quickly, and it broke. They took him to the emergency clinic right away and operated on him. I never saw him again. A couple of months later, the operations sergeant arrived. Everyone started having problems with him because he was arrogant and bossy.

One Sunday morning, a boy named Oscar and I overslept and didn't go to classes. Actually, it wasn't mandatory to attend that class. The teacher was maybe going to lecture that day. To avoid being found, Oscar and I preferred to go to some orange groves near the camp. We left early and returned before sunset. The operations sergeant was waiting for us, very upset.

"Where have you been all day?" he said to us in a loud and

commanding voice. "You didn't go to today's class! But know that you're going to pay for it. I'll take care of that!"

"Sergeant," I replied in the same manner as him. "Today is Sunday, and it's not mandatory to attend that class, and we decided to take our day off like every Sunday!"

He was so furious that he lunged at me, trying to grab me by the shoulder and push me with an almost mechanical movement. I ducked and tripped him with my feet between his. We started throwing punches, and I, with more agility and less height than him, took the lead. He tried to hit me with one of his blows, but didn't succeed. A few soldiers came to separate us. I was so angry that they had to give me a hard blow to the head, and I lost consciousness.

When I woke up, I was in a cell at the camp. I found out that charges were being brought against me, and there was already a legal case because I had knocked out the sergeant's front teeth and fractured his arm. Three days later, they took me out of the cell. The comrades who saw how it all started supported me. They dropped the charges, and as a punishment, I was suspended from going home. Every six months, they gave us a pass to go home and be with our families. And I lost it because of my bad behavior.

At the camp, I had quite a bit of fun; there were companions doing strange things. One day after lunch, instead of going to work, a friend and I decided to go for a horseback ride and then visit our girlfriends. We entered the stables and saw a companion on a rock, with his back turned and his pants down.

"Arturo, look! Who could that be?" I said with curiosity to my friend.

"I don't know, Ronaldito!" he said with a malicious tone. "Let's get closer to see what's going on. Shh! Don't make a fuss," I told him.

The closer we got, we saw horse legs next to the rock and saw that guy making love to the mare.

"Arturo, let's scare him so he stops being so shameless," my friend exclaimed and I forcefully. The guy got so scared that he jumped and quickly got off the rock without pulling up his pants. He ran so fast that he touched his backside with his heels. We laughed so hard that, although we tried to run faster, we could never catch him. Arturo, my friend, peed his pants, and we forgot the reason we were going.

We returned to the camp, and just as we arrived, the pre-combat alarm went off. We ran to present ourselves. All the recruits lined up, and the sergeants and captains began to arrive.

"Recruits! We have news received by telegram. It informs us that all those recruits from here who want to be close to this place must cut fifty arrobas of cane each. If they succeed, they will be transferred to the one in Matanzas, the closest to Havana. Those who want their transfer, take two steps forward."

I don't remember how many of us stepped forward, but there were quite a few. They gave us machetes and hoes.

"Recruits! The tools we gave you are for cleaning the camp today and storing them to cut the cane tomorrow. Understood?"

We started working by cutting the grass that was already very tall. They gave me two machetes.

"Rolando! Hey, Rolando!" I heard someone shouting at me and turned to see who it was.

"What do you say, Socarra?" I responded, looking at a comrade who was three feet away and whom we always called by his last name.

"Throw me one of the machetes you have," he said.

"No, better come get it because I can't throw it to you."

"Throw it to me, I tell you, and stop the nonsense."

I took the machete and threw it to him as he asked. When the machete was near him, Socarra jumped, and before it hit the ground, it struck his foot right above the heel, breaking his tendon.

"I can't walk, my foot is not responding. If you had listened to me, I would have gone for the machete myself."

"I'm sorry, I didn't throw it intentionally. It's okay, I know," I replied with a pained expression.

We called the sergeant and when he saw it, he quickly took him to the hospital. After that accident, the young man did not return.

It was seven in the morning, the sun was shining brightly. It was very hot, the place was arid, and the wind was blowing gently without refreshing. The sugarcane fields, seen from afar, didn't seem so large, but inside they were enormous. I thought we would never manage to cut the fifty loads of cane.

Despite the heat, we started working very well. Around one in the afternoon, I started to feel very unwell and decided to go to where the sergeants were to tell them what was happening to me. They ignored me and I had a terrible headache. I returned to work and couldn't continue anymore, so I went back to the sergeants and told them I felt bad. It seems my demeanor was depressing.

"It's okay, kid," they told me. "You already have your pass to transfer to Matanzas. Go back to the unit."

I left immediately. I went straight to my bed and lay down. I slept for a while, but the discomfort woke me up. I had a headache, chest pain, and back pain. Later my comrades arrived and told me to pack my things because we would be transferred to Matanzas that same day. Eight o'clock in the evening came and we were told to line up. A loudspeaker called us by name to board the bus. When they called me, I wanted to take my things but I couldn't. A comrade helped me with my bags. I was about to board the bus when everything went dark and I knew no more.

I remember seeing an intense white light that illuminated me from afar and it was getting closer. I heard people speaking to me, but the voices sounded distant. I couldn't do anything, I felt calm and happy.

I woke up and saw that I was in a white room. I looked around and saw that to the right of the bed there was a table. On the left side, there was a tube from which hung a transparent bag containing a liquid similar to water. From the bag hung a thin cord of the same color. I also saw another cord coming from my nose and mouth. There were other devices that scared me when I saw them.

"Doctor, what happened to me?" I asked.

"You got triple pneumonia. You almost died, you have been unconscious for seven days. What you have in your hand is serum."

"And what about everything else I have in my mouth and nose?"

"You have oxygen and a tube for spitting out saliva."

"And the devices?"

"They are to measure your blood pressure, temperature, heart, etc. Stop talking, you'll get better in a few more days."

Days after regaining consciousness, they returned me to Camagüey. Returning to the camp wasn't the same for me, and I didn't want to be there.

An idea occurred to me and I went to look for sap and sandpaper. I hid among the bushes, rubbed the top of my feet with the wood sandpaper, and then applied the sap pulp. Finally, I put on my socks and shoes. The next day, I woke up with swollen feet. The sergeant took me to the hospital. I did this several times until they eventually discharged me from the army.

3
THE EMBASSY

"Ronaldito, what are you doing here?! Why are you only coming to see us now? It's been three months since the pass given, and you didn't come."

"No mom, I didn't come because I had problems. But I'm not going back to the army, I've been discharged."

"What? How did you get discharged?"

"Silvia, look, I'll tell you everything that happened to me." One day later, when I finished telling everything, my mom was more at ease.

"Look mom, this envelope has my retirement paper inside."

"It's better if you don't return. I feel more relieved."

"Mom, what happened to Carlitos?" I asked my mother, curiously.

"Carlitos went to the United States."

"What? To the United States?" I replied, very surprised.

"Yes son, he went to that country."

I remained very thoughtful about what my mother told me. I felt like leaving too.

"My mom's boyfriend found me a job, helping to change tires on buses. I took the opportunity to take some tubes home and with those, I started to build a little boat."

I decided to escape. That day the sky was a deep blue, there were no clouds. The sun was shining and the breeze was fresh. The sea was calm. The waves gently rocked my little boat.

"I started rowing quickly. I hadn't even gone two miles when the coast guards saw me and began approaching where I was. Meanwhile, I took the opportunity to throw some cans of food I had brought and kept a few threads and hooks for fishing."

"What are you doing here, boy?" the coast guards questioned me doubtfully.

"I'm fishing," I answered.

"Well, it doesn't seem like it," they said, "because you were quite far from the beach, don't you think?"

"Well, I was just fishing."

"Well, look, you have to come with us."

They took me to shore and wanted to accuse me of treason, but since there was no evidence that I wanted to escape, they decided to call my mom. They complained about me and then let me go.

"Ronaldito! Tell me the truth," my mother said to me.

"About what, mom?"

"It's true that you want to leave this country, right?"

"Yes mom, I do want to leave here. You know we live in poverty and in this country, we're going nowhere. We've spent Christmases without having what other countries have. Also, Christmas is forbidden here."

"Look son, I love you very much and I don't want to lose you. But if you've already decided to leave, I respect that. The only thing I tell you is not to do it that way. There are other ways to leave this country without risking your life. I'm telling you from experience."

Those days were too hot. Anyone would like to go to the beach and have fun. I wanted to go fishing. I remember very well that it was Thursday. I waited for Reynaldo and Mayito and they didn't show up. They had to go get firewood for their house, as back then many families didn't have a stove to cook. Besides, one had to invent ways to get food because the government quota wasn't enough for the whole month.

We planned between talks, jokes, and games to go fishing the next day. We were already adults. Rey was seventeen, Mayito twenty-two, and I was twenty years old.

That Friday my mom woke me up at four in the morning so I would accompany her to her work. She had to pick up some things for me to bring home. I got up very happily because when I went to my mom's work, she would prepare me a nice meal and give me some ham; in that kitchen, they had everything since it was government-owned. That day my mom gave me rice, beans, bread, etc. I took the things home. Around eleven in the morning, my stepfather arrived home. I was in the kitchen, sitting on a chair. My stepfather started chatting with me while having lunch.

"Have you already heard what happened at the Peruvian Embassy with the Cuban government?" he said to me.

"No, what happened? Tell me."

"Well, you see, the Cuban government is in a dispute with the Peruvian Embassy because some Cubans took a bus and forcibly entered the Embassy with all their family. With all the commotion they caused, a guard escorting the Embassy died. The Peruvian ambassadors are protecting the people who started the trouble. They don't want to hand them over; they say it's a shame not to investigate how things happened because the Castro government wants to make them pay for the crime without knowing if they're guilty or not."

"And what does Castro say about that?" I asked.

"You know how they are. It seems he ordered to remove the guards from the Embassy."

"I don't know where that embassy is," I told him. "Surely by investigating, I'll get there. I'll see what happened, and if possible, I'll go in. Look, I'm going to check it out."

"Be very careful, boy. If the situation is bad, you better come back home." I stood up from the chair, went towards the room where my brother and I slept. At the threshold of the room door, my brother caught up with me. He had been listening to the conversation between my stepfather and me.

"I'm going with you," my brother said to me, "don't leave me here."

"Look," I replied, "I'm going with the intention of fishing. If I happen to find out where the Peruvian Embassy street is, I'll investigate first what happened. If there's a chance to leave the country, I'll take you with me."

My brother, with what I told him, remained very confident. I knew it wasn't going to be easy. I thought that if I were to die in my attempt, it would only be me. That way my mother would only suffer for one son, not both. I was thinking about the Embassy when I heard someone knocking on the door. I went to open it. It was the gentlemen with whom I started working delivering bread after the coastguards caught me in my escape attempt.

"Ronaldito, let's go to work!" they said to me. "Maybe we'll finish earlier today if we hurry."

"Today I can't go with you. I have to run a very important errand for my mom."

"But, how? Mmmh, that's fine," they said. "Will you be free tomorrow?"

"Yes, tomorrow I will."

"Then, we'll come by at the same time."

"Alright. I'll be ready at that time."

Half an hour later my friends Rey and Mayito arrived. The day was hot and there was almost no breeze. We wanted to go to the seafront to fish. We were walking along the coastal avenue and in the distance, we saw a lot of people. None of us paid it any attention and we continued on our way. We reached a place called 'la punta'. The blue sky was reflected in the water. We sat on the rocks, prepared our lines and hooks to fish. I was thinking about the Embassy. After a while, we decided to return. We were walking and saw that people were still on that street. I thought of approaching the place.

"Guys, let's go over there! Let's see why all those people are there, something must be happening!"

"Yes, let's go!" Rey replied. "Maybe they're handing out things.

The closer we got, we realized something was happening. We didn't know if it was something good, so we started to ask what was going on.

"Excuse me, sir! Hey, sir!"

"What do you want, boy?"

"Why are there so many people? What happened?"

"Here is where people got into the embassy. Well, it's the Peruvian Embassy. Seems like someone died, you know." My heart raced upon hearing that, although I already suspected it. I never imagined it was that Embassy.

"Guys! Did you hear that?"

"Yes, Rolando, we heard."

"Well, look, I want to get into the Embassy, to leave this country."

"Us too," Mario said.

I remember it was April seventeenth, nineteen eighty, when we entered. We were all getting into the Embassy, and others were finding out what had happened. We took advantage of a space between the people who were looking through the broken fence in front of the Embassy and got in through that place. Once inside, we started to talk about what we would do if we left the country. I never thought about what would happen afterward. It was noon, and we saw that Fidel's government had removed the guards from the Embassy.

The Embassy covered a whole block. The two sides and back of the Embassy bordered streets. And the front bordered the avenue along the shoreline of the seafront. I remember the left side, the back, and the front of the Embassy were covered by a fence about six feet high. The right side was covered by a cement wall approximately eight feet high. In the middle of the wall was an iron gate through which cars entered, following a circuit that surrounded the building and ended at the same gate. At the back, there was a garden with about eighteen fruit trees.

The Embassy generally had, on each of its four corners, plus a small room, from which the escort guards watched. The building had a balcony on the second floor facing the garden, and at the front, there was only the entrance, which consisted of a regular-sized door with a small three-step staircase, and on the second floor, two windows. It was separated from the front fence by twelve or thirteen feet. Below, the building had three windows, and above, also three.

I stood by the left side fence. People kept entering, and the place was getting full. Perhaps it was six in the evening when the soldiers arrived. They began to clear the place and did not let more people enter. Immediately after, they surrounded the entire Embassy. They carried, what a bad memory, high-caliber rifles.

Suddenly, and without knowing from where, I heard gunshots. Next to me was a lady who was six or seven months pregnant. I turned and saw a car coming quickly directly towards the broken mesh in front of the Embassy.

Inside were three gentlemen shooting at the soldiers. They were trying to enter the Embassy. At that moment, I tried to cover the lady beside me, but it was in vain because she was hit by a bullet that struck her stomach.

I felt an enormous despair when I saw her bleed abundantly. I called for help. Within seconds, some men took her inside the Embassy and I never knew anything else about her.

While one of the men in the car managed to get inside, the other two were taken by the police. After the incident, I moved from the place where I was and went to a safer area. That day we didn't sleep at all because there was a tremendous uproar inside and outside the Embassy. The place where I stayed was next to the wall. I settled there and thought about how, when I was a child, I dreamed of having nice pants or lived with the illusion of having a toy. But that just stayed in my dreams.

The place was so crowded that you couldn't even walk.

April eighteenth, in the morning. We had nothing to eat and we didn't sleep because there was no space to do so. In a corner of the Embassy was a water basin, and people formed a very long line to get water. There was a hot sun. My friends and I stood under a tree for its shade.

For a minute I thought the government would send us food. It didn't happen. That first day passed without positive news about what they were going to do with us.

April nineteenth. It was already the second day and my friends Rey and Mayito were desperate. The heat felt more suffocating because there were too many of us.

"Ronaldito, we're hungry! Let's find food no matter what," said Mayito.

"Wait a bit," I replied. "I don't think they'll leave us hungry all day. They have to provide a solution."

"I hope that's true," replied Rey.

That day they kept nagging. Hearing them so much, I too started getting hungry. I began to devise what to do to calm the hunger a little. I saw the trees nearby and they were mango trees, but their fruit was not yet ready to eat.

"Look, if you're so hungry!" I said to them somewhat insolently. "Start eating mangos, that'll curb your hunger a little."

"Rolando!" Mayito replied. "Don't you see it's still April and the mango is very green? You can't eat it."

"Well look, go ahead and eat them. Maybe if they make you sick, you'll stop bothering me. Why do you think I have the obligation to feed you? If that's the case, I don't know from where I'm supposed to get the food."

That day it was already evening and we hadn't eaten anything. I climbed the mango tree and started eating the green fruits. My friends saw me eating so eagerly that they did the same. And then, the people around us started eating even the leaves.

Outside, people didn't want to go home. The guards making sure people didn't keep entering had closed the streets. Inside the Embassy, those talking started all the bustle, conversing with the ambassadors to know what solution Castro would give to our situation.

We heard voices from people looking for their relatives who were inside there.

April twentieth, what a terrible day, there was a humid heat. We were all hungry and still, there was no solution. Around noon, a man came out onto the Embassy's balcony with a loudspeaker asking for our attention. I peeked through the crowd to see if I could spot who it was. However, there were so many of us that we seemed like worms in that tiny place.

"Compatriots, I want you to pay attention," he told us. I never thought things would get so complicated. "Look, everything started when I heard that Peru and Cuba were discussing the human rights violations here in Cuba. You know how Fidel is; he got so upset that he immediately ordered the guards watching the Embassy to be removed. So, I took a bus and brought all my family. I headed to this place and when I arrived, I saw the guards were still watching. My first impulse was to drive the bus against the fence in front of the embassy. I didn't expect to be shot at. As I passed by the watchtower on the right corner at the front, a guard came out and fired at the bus. The bullet ricocheted and hit another guard, who was killed."

"Compatriots, I had no revolver, I swear! But... you know the Cuban government doesn't investigate. They just come and kill you. And I don't want to die, because it took a lot of effort to get here just to lose my life in a minute and never get to know what it feels like to be free!"

"Compatriots, among you, there are some companions handing out sheets of paper. Please, write down your name and return the papers to the companions, because the ambassadors are going to talk with Castro's government to get us food. Don't be swayed by what people outside are saying! It's just to scare you so you don't leave. In other countries, it's not like here..."

While he was talking, we finished signing up and they started counting how many we were. In total, we were ten thousand five hundred people. The representative continued talking, and the people outside were listening, because they immediately started throwing stones, sticks, and everything they could find. We tried to cover each other and also took shelter under the trees. Even so, many ended up with head injuries. In the commotion, some elderly people ended up with broken arms or legs. The Peruvian Embassy did everything possible to help us, but it wasn't enough as they were overwhelmed with medical service cases.

At night, everyone was hungry. The trees were without mangoes or leaves. Some gentlemen cut the leaves off some plants, whose names I don't know, to make a tea. They went inside the Embassy to ask for some metal buckets and later boiled the leaves in water. Everyone nearby drank that tea and it gave us a lot of energy, allowing us to get through the night.

It was close to midnight when those outside started throwing stones at us. A guard who was near us on the outside, with complete cynicism, was able to call out by name to one of those attacking us.

“Hey, Leopoldo! Look, be careful!” said the guard. “Don't hit me!”

“Don't worry! I know what I'm doing.”

The guard knew they were people from the same government. It was dark, and we didn't know where the stones would come from. A woman fell, and as she did, a stone hit her on the head. There was too much blood, but she was so angry that she didn't care.

“Long live freedom!” she began to shout, despite being hurt. “Long live freedom! You won't defeat me! I'd rather be dead than go back with you!”

We, who saw her, spoke to her to protect herself.

“Come, come ma'am! Because they'll hit you again! Protect yourself.”

She came to where we were, and we took her to the plants nearby. We tried to make her comfortable. Meanwhile, I went to ask for help. They took her inside the Embassy.

It was almost dawn when things started to calm down a bit.

April twenty-first: It was the fourth day, and I started chatting with my friends about what we would do when we were free.

“But I don't know why we're talking about this,” commented Rey, “when we don't know if we'll leave this place alive or dead.”

“Look, I don't know what you all think,” I told them, “but in my opinion, I think we're going to triumph and be able to do what we've never done in this country. So stop thinking nonsense and think that we'll come out of this situation well.”

I was sure we were going to leave the country. I tried to advise them and also encouraged them so they wouldn't regret it. That day passed quietly.

April twenty-second: That morning, people didn't bother us. I, tired of being in the same place all night, decided to walk a bit. A few feet away, I saw some men listening to the news on a small radio. I tried to get closer but couldn't hear anything, so I decided to wait for the news to be repeated to see if they said something about our situation. But I couldn't find out anything. People were crowded around the radio.

“Sir, did you hear anything?” I asked a man who was coming out from the crowd.

“I heard that Raúl Castro said he would come this afternoon. That he would talk to us.”

“Ah, we'll see if he comes,” I answered incredulously.

I wondered what their plans were because outside, people were still throwing things at us, and the soldiers pretended to calm the people, but they wouldn't listen. They shouted at us to repent for what we were doing, to come out of there.

I wasn't going to give up or let myself be defeated. My strong desire to be free told me that I had to endure.

Even though hunger sometimes tried to dominate us, I tried to always stand firm. I needed to keep going.

In the afternoon of that day, Raúl Castro arrived. He stood in front of the embassy. He started talking, and as I suspected, he began to say that we shouldn't be foolish, to return to our homeland with our family, etc. For me, those were the most stupid words he spoke. Most expected him to tell us we could go to another country, to propose something more positive, to solve our situation.

I didn't want to hear anymore and decided to sleep while people listened to what he was saying.

"Ronaldito, wake up!" my friend Rey said to me.

"Huh? What's going on? Has Raúl Castro and his people left?"

"Yes, they left. You slept for like three hours."

"That long? Hey, what did he say?"

"Well, he said he was going to send us food. Only for five thousand people."

"Mmmh... I hope it's true. Hey, but you realize," I told Rey, "that he will only send for five thousand if we are ten thousand five hundred people. Look, what they want is for us to fight each other so that we destroy ourselves. Then they will have an excuse for the world. No one will tell them that they killed us, but that we ended ourselves, and no one will know that what is happening is a reflection of the disagreement between the people and the government because of the political system that was forced upon us."

"Could it be true, Ronaldito?" he asked me with a lot of curiosity.

"Think about it," I replied. "This is a shame! The system says there are no poor people, that we are all equal! And there is no freedom of expression! And I don't know what else! That's why they'd rather see us dead than let us leave Cuba.

April twenty-third: That day dawned a little cool, and we continued talking about the government system in our country. Around two in the afternoon, a gentleman jumped in from the balcony overlooking the garden and with a loudspeaker told us there was food.

"Compatriots! Pay attention!" he said to us. "We have food. It is little, so we will first distribute it to children and the elderly, then to women, and if there's any left, to all the men who are left!"

We all agreed. That was another day without eating. I already felt weak, but I did my best to hold on so as not to... Especially knowing that if we managed to get out of the country, my life would change. We thought about walking along the edge of the garden, close to the fence surrounding the Embassy, and suddenly a cat appeared.

"Why don't we catch that cat?" Rey said. "And eat it! Don't you think, Rolando?"

"You're crazy!" I replied.

"It's a little animal. If you don't catch it, I'll catch it myself!" he said.

"But we have nothing to cook it!" I answered.

"Don't worry. There's always a way to do things. You just have to look."

"Alright," I said, "then let's hurry if you don't want our meal to get away."

Mario stood by one side of the fence lifting it, and I hid behind him, and threw some fish bones I found in the Embassy's garden. Rey was calling it. When I threw the bones, the cat came to eat them. At that moment, Rey pulled it so quickly that its skin got caught on the fence. We felt sad for the little animal. The cat died immediately. We prepared to find something to finish skinning it. I decided to go ask who had a knife.

An old man who was chatting around had one. I approached him with some embarrassment.

"Sir, can we borrow your knife?" I said.

"What do you want it for, boy?" he asked.

"To finish skinning that cat because we just caught it."

"Yes, boy, I'll lend it to you," he replied, "but tell me one thing. Are you going to eat that cat without inviting me? Because I am also very hungry!"

I felt more confident when the man told me that.

"I thought you were going to scold us for killing that cat. But I see you're not, and when you're hungry and in a situation like this, you eat whatever you can."

The man came over to where we were and helped us clean the cat. That day I felt filled with happiness because after so many days of not eating anything, the little animal was delicious. The people around us were amazed. They looked at us in disbelief. Some even said we were crazy.

The people outside had not bothered us for three days, and I was getting my hopes up that everything was calming down.

April twenty-fourth: It was the same routine. The food was still being distributed to women, children, and the elderly. If there was any left, they gave it to the rest of us. I got one and shared it with my companions.

April twenty-fifth: That day it was Rey and Mayito's turn for food. They invited the man who lent us the knife and me. That man became very good friends with us since we shared the cat, and after that, we shared the food whenever it was our turn.

April twenty-sixth: A few people came by outside, they didn't bother us. They looked at us very insistently, perhaps waiting for us to regret it and abandon the idea of leaving Cuba.

It was the ninth day, and Rey and his brother were desperate.

"We can't take it anymore!" Rey said.

"Now that we're already inside," I told him, "and after nine days, you want to leave? You're crazy! You're going to leave me alone! I can't believe it!"

"Look, Ronaldito," Mayito said to me, "if they give us a chance to go home to eat something and then come back, do you think they'd let us enter again?"

"No, I don't think they'd let you."

"What if we try?" Rey asked.

"I don't think so. Either way, I'm not going anywhere."

"Why?" Mayito asked.

"No, I will stay here until death. Look, I want to know how all this ends. I imagine the government will make a deal with those from Peru. Although honestly, I am somewhat confused."

That afternoon, our representative went out to the balcony to communicate the arrangements that the Ambassador was making with Castro's people.

"Fellow countrymen! I want you to listen to me and pay close attention to what I am going to tell you!" he said to us in a very loud voice. "A candidate will come to provide safe-conducts to all the people who want to go home to get food. If you want, you can return! They assure us there is no problem!"

When we heard those words, we all started making comments about it.

"Could it be true?" some said. "And... what if we go and can't come back?"

"I'm hungry," said others. "And if I go home and come back here..."

Rey and Mayito were very happy.

"Ronaldito! Did you hear?" Rey said to me. "Let's go home! We just eat and then come back!"

"Well, look, guajiro," I told them, "because this seems very strange to me. It could be a trap by Fidel Castro!"

"No, that can't be," Rey replied. "The representative is guaranteeing it for us! I think it's something safe!"

I remained thoughtful, and not convinced to go home and return. That was not possible! Why, then, were there so many guards?

"Fellow countrymen!" the representative continued. "I know that all of you are suffering more than those of us inside here! That's why I ask you for strength to endure. We have to emerge victorious from this struggle! I repeat again that you shouldn't listen to the people outside. They only think about their communism, not about being free one day! We are in this place fighting for a future that Fidel Castro always promised us! And it's already been twenty years and we still haven't seen anything! We have to continue fighting to achieve that future on our own. Remember that they throw everything they find at us, but it's to provoke us! If we respond to those aggressions, it's certain that the soldiers, using that excuse, will shoot at us. And in that way, little by little, they will finish us off!"

April 27: That day they returned with the same comments about the safe-conducts. The people who decided to leave approached those who were going to give the safe-conducts.

My friends Rey and Mayito decided to leave and waited for a few people to go first to make sure it was true. I was very sad because they gave up. When I saw that they were leaving, I felt like crying because they were going to leave me alone. I hugged them with deep emotion because I knew I wouldn't see them again. I thought 'if that's their decision, go ahead. Hopefully, nothing happens to them on their way home'. They lined up to get their paper. I noticed they were given some papers that looked like letters, they showed them to me from afar. I couldn't see what they said. Apparently, they seemed invalid. Later I found out that they were indeed not valid and that they were only given to the people to make them leave the Embassy. Few people had left. The rest of us decided to stay until the end.

A man who was giving the safe-conducts started talking to us.

"We want you to decide! Believe us: The people will not do anything to you! If you decide to leave here for your homes, we guarantee that nothing will happen to you! Or what do you want so that you believe what we are telling you?"

Immediately, one of us spoke up.

"We want President Fidel Castro to come personally to speak with us!"

"That will never happen!" replied the Castrist candidate. "Because Mr. President Fidel Castro sent us as his representatives. That's why we come on his behalf to give you a last opportunity!"

None of us wanted to move from the place. The few people who accepted the safe-conduct numbered around one hundred and fifty. The rest, despite our hunger, decided to stay there, even if we were dying, but we wanted something certain.

April 28: When we thought no one was going to bother us anymore, some small vans started arriving, which, if I remember correctly, were vans that only the government used and they were new. My dad had one of those vans and he worked for the government. The town only had old cars. The vans arrived filled with people who, upon getting off, began walking around the Embassy. They finally stopped in front of the main door of the building. They started speaking through a loudspeaker. I climbed a tree to see the person speaking. I couldn't see him from below. There were too many people. I was weak because I hadn't eaten enough. I tried to stay there for a while and listened to what they were saying.

"We suggest you go home!" shouted the man speaking, "Because the commanders of Cuba promise you nothing! You're starving here! You're uncomfortable!"

It was almost six in the afternoon. Those people kept circling the Embassy. I was tired and decided to get down from the tree. I saw a boy, maybe fifteen years old, climb up it. About ten seconds later, I saw him fall like he was a little bird. Someone from outside threw a rock that hit his head. The boy lost consciousness. The guards who were watching us from outside laughed as if what they did to the young boy was funny. Some men picked him up and took him inside the Embassy. I reflected on my good luck because I had been in that tree for quite some time and nothing had happened to me.

"Thank you, my God! Because nothing happened to me, but help the boy because he has done no harm!"

I don't know how I made that prayer since I never went to church. When Fidel Castro took the presidency in Cuba, he immediately ordered them to close (as my mother told me).

After that unpleasant incident, I decided not to climb any more trees, and also avoided getting too close to the fence or the wall. That night I couldn't sleep because people here started throwing rocks, sticks, and other things they could find at us. Additionally, they yelled at us:

GET OUT, WORMS, GET OUT BECAUSE
WE DON'T WANT TO ROT!

When I heard those people shouting like that, it gave me hope that we would leave the country and I felt stronger. That day I couldn't take it anymore; I was so hungry that I decided to cut some grass and eat it. As it was so bitter, I went to line up to get some water. There were many people, everyone tried to feel less hungry by drinking water. The trees offered no shade, they were leafless. The heat was unbearable. There was no place to lie down for a moment and rest.

The afternoon was arriving when the people outside decided to leave.

April 29: The morning was fresh. The seagulls passed several times over us. Some people arrived, whom we knew. They were police. However, there they were dressed as civilians, they threw papers at us that said:

DOWN WITH THE ESCORT TRAITORS!
LONG LIVE COMMUNISM!
AND YOU LEAVE!

When I picked up one of those papers and read what it said, I was very happy because it said "you leave." Although we really didn't know if we were leaving or not.

Between one and two in the afternoon, Raúl Castro appeared and gave us a solution.

"Listen, everyone! We guarantee you the visa, a safe passage, and the passport. With those documents, you will leave for other countries that have granted you political asylum. But those who entered by force will not be given papers because a revolutionary brother died because of them, and those people have to pay for it."

Raúl Castro was there, giving us a solution to our problem. Nobody could believe it. Some people started to line up to get their papers. I thought "I'd better hold on one more day. I'm not sure. I don't care I'm so weak from hunger. I want to be convinced that I'm going to obtain my freedom."

I waited until the rest of the day passed. It was almost eight at night, and around two thousand people had already left with their papers.

I started feeling more confident and waited until the next day.

April 30: That day it was almost ten in the morning, and Raúl Castro's people hadn't arrived. I thought they wouldn't come back. But what was going to happen to all of us?

At eleven in the morning, they arrived, and people started lining up. After three hours, I decided to look for my papers.

When I reached the table where they were giving out the documents, they asked me a very foolish question.

"Do you want to leave the country?"

"Yes, why?"

"Don't you know this is treason?"

"I don't know if it's treason or not, but I want to leave the country to have a future."

The man got very upset when I answered like that, so he grabbed my papers and tossed them at me.

"Enough with the arguments! Get over to the next table! They'll give you the address where you need to go to finish getting your exit. And get out! Before I regret it and change my mind."

I took my papers and headed to the next table. They gave me an address that was near where my aunt lived. The neighborhood is called Marianao. There's a beach there called El Náutico. I took the address and got ready to leave. It occurred to me to hide the papers in my underwear.

4
THE TRAP

With the firm idea of not trusting anyone, I left the embassy. The people on the sidewalks looked at us as if we were murderers or something like that. It was all because we wanted to leave the country. When I started to walk, I realized that everything was planned. It was a trap!

My firm decision to free myself filled me with courage. Hunger drove me to walk to get home. The more I walked, something inside me told me to stay alert.

The way people were, I knew that at any moment someone would hit me. The hardest part was that they made us walk on the sidewalk among the people. At every corner, we had to show our papers to the guards, who asked us to display our documents. When we showed them, the people keeping watch knew who we were and that we were leaving. Then they shouted a series of things at us, pushed us, and threw stones.

When I reached the second to last corner, they asked me to show my papers. I saw that there were a lot of people and some distracted the guards. I showed my documents and put them back in my underwear. I don't know where a tall, burly man came from and hit me behind the ear, knocking me to the ground. I realized immediately and got up quickly, running as fast as I could. I passed by a policeman, who did nothing to stop the people.

"Hey, kid," the policeman shouted at me, "this isn't a place to run! If you did this, now you have to pay! Because I didn't tell you to go into the embassy!" I kept running. Passing through the crowd, they clung to me from all sides. My desperation was such that I was looking for a way out. I realized there were fewer people there compared to the earlier streets. I reached the last corner and noticed there weren't as many guards.

They asked for my papers, and I showed them, putting them back in my underwear. I felt a tremendous blow to the back of my head and fell to the ground headfirst. The person who hit me was tall and strong. They dragged me along the sidewalk. I tried in vain to get up because other people kicked and punched me from all sides.

"Here come more!" shouted one of my aggressors.

They were referring to the people who left the embassy after me. Some stopped hitting me. It was a moment I took advantage of to escape so fast that they couldn't catch me. I ran across the avenue until I reached a bridge where I used to sleep when I went fishing at night. I stayed there for more than an hour until I felt better. I went out to look for a bus to take me home. When I got on the bus, people looked at me strangely. For a moment, I thought they would hit me too. I tried to pretend I was crazy to avoid them doing something to me.

I reached home and knocked on the door. I fainted.

I woke up and my mom was beside me.

"Mom?" I asked, a bit disoriented, thinking I was still in the embassy.

"Yes, son, I'm here."

"Mom, I'm glad I'm here. Who opened the door for me?"

"Your sister, and you were unconscious. I was scared because you've been like that for two days," she said. "I found out from the neighbors that you went into the embassy!"

"Yes, and I feel proud! Even if I'm all beaten up! I don't care! Look, I already have the safe-conduct! And also this address, so you and dad can come with me and give your authorization for me to leave the country!"

"Our authorization?"

"Yes, the address they gave is near the beach at El Náutico, where my aunt lives. They're going to give us some papers there for you and dad to sign, giving me authorization to leave Cuba. Don't you remember I haven't reached the age of majority yet?"

"Yes, son, you're right! But tell me, where are your visa and passport?"

"They'll give them to me once you sign the papers I'm telling you about."

"I hope so. You see how this government is, today they tell you one thing... tomorrow they do another. Be careful and don't say anything because they'll arrest you and accuse you of who knows how many things. Son, that's why I pray to God to help you leave this country. So you can experience freedom, just like I did years ago. So many that I don't even remember! Well, I'd better keep my mouth shut and go to the kitchen to make you some soup because look how weak you are."

"Mamacita," I asked as she headed to the kitchen, "what happened with Rey and Mayito? I want to go see them."

"Son, if you don't want to get into more trouble with the government, don't go anywhere! Look, they broke Reynaldo's foot and Mayito was beaten so badly that he's still in the hospital."

After what my mom told me, I was very thoughtful. She was right! I didn't know how things were outside my house. No one had seen me arrive. I was hiding until the day I had my appointment at the Nautico. That day I had to wear a suit to take my passport photo.

My mother, who had some savings, went to buy me the suit. She went to the store with my measurements written in a notebook and bought me the clothes, which were too big for me.

"Son, look at the suit I bought you," she said, "try it on."

"Mom, it's too big," I said when I finished putting on those clothes.

"You're right," she said, a little thoughtful.

"And now how do we fix it?" I asked anxiously.

"Don't worry, son. Tonight we are going to your grandma's house and she will fix it for you. Meanwhile, I'll go with your father to convince him to come with us to the Nautico to sign the papers."

My father was a government judge. At first, he told my mother he would sign them. When my mother came back days later to give him the date and time we had to be at the Nautico, my father said he wouldn't sign anymore.

"You know... I'm not going to sign the papers," my father said.

"What do you mean you're not going to sign them?" my mother replied. "Why?"

"I don't know how my work colleagues found out. Yesterday they had a meeting with me and told me that if I signed the papers, I couldn't continue being a judge. Do you know what that means?"

"And you're more worried about your 'position' than your own son?"

"You know that..."

"No! I only know that you have to sign those papers," my mom told him. "Please, I beg you to sign the papers because I don't want to lose my son. If he stays in the country, they are going to kill him! The people in the neighborhood don't even want to see him! They say they don't want any traitors around! That they would rather kill him!"

After my mom begged him for two days, my father agreed to sign my documents.

"Ah, is that you? Come in," my mom told him. "Your son is coming now."

"He should hurry, so we have time to do everything necessary."

"I’m ready. Let's go!" I told them.

We left in a government truck. They gave it to my father to use as transportation because his job required him to be in various places. With that truck, he went from one place to another without wasting time.

We arrived at the Nautico beach. There were many people waiting for those of us leaving the country. We got out of the truck and started walking. People began to shout at us. My father, hearing them, got nervous. My mother tried to calm him down.

GO AWAY, GO AWAY!
WE DON'T WANT YOU HERE!

"Stay calm. Nothing is going to happen here," my mother told my father. "Keep walking without looking around."

"But they could hit us!" my father replied, very nervous. "Look how upset they are!"

"Don't look at them. Keep going," my mom told him bravely. "Don't show fear."

That day I thought that going with my father might make me feel calmer. However, he was more scared than I was. He knew that the people shouting at us were sent by the government and were willing to hit us. That's why he was afraid. We entered the offices and there was a very long line.

"Why did you do this, boy?" my father asked me angrily. "We wouldn't be going through all this! You know you're harming your mother and me! Now, look at all those people! I'm worried because they are very aggressive. Your mom says not to look anywhere! But I can't help it!"

"Don't ask me, because you never cared for me and now that I really need you, you're not supporting me," I replied.

"I'm asking you because now I'm worried about all this."

"Well, it's not right that you're only worried now. Look, a father fights for his son until the end, no matter what he does in life, even if it's the last thing."

"But what you did is not worthy of support! How do you want to leave the country where you were born and raised? Do you think I would give my life for that?"

"Oh, it's true. You're right! You've been dead since you became a communist. A dead man can't support anyone because he has neither voice nor vote. It's true!"

My father was very restless, and we entered into a discussion. My mother tried to calm us.

"I'll leave and won't sign anything!" my father said suddenly.

"No! No! Please, calm down. Nothing is going to happen. Just sign, and if you want, you can leave afterwards!"

"Don't worry, Mom," I told her. "He is in here and he has to sign. If he doesn't, I'll run out and shout that he also wants to leave, and that he belongs to the government! He knows what they'll do to him!"

My dad had no choice but to endure. When we reached the counter, they gave us several papers that he signed. I felt a great relief. They told my parents that I couldn't leave my house for four or five days because the State security would come for me and take me to the place from where I would leave the country. They gave me the visa, the safe-conduct, and the passport. My father was too upset, but he still took us home.

Three days later, at eleven-thirty in the morning, there was a knock on the door.

"Does Rolando Castillo live here?" one of the two policemen asked my sister.

"Yes, he lives here," my sister replied, who had opened the door for them.

"Tell him to come quickly because we don't have time, and he has to leave the country."

I heard what they said to my sister and went out. They quickly put me in the car they were driving. They took me to an airport near the Peruvian Embassy.

"Look, kid, we're going to take you to Miramar airport. You're going to catch the flight to Spain," they told me as we headed to the airport. "The plane leaves at twelve sharp. And from where we drop you off, you have to run quickly to catch it."

"But it's almost twelve already!"

"Well, see what you're going to do because, hmm..." he said as he looked at his watch, "fifteen minutes left. And by the time we get there... well, you have three to four little minutes to catch the flight."

When he told me how much time I had, I thought: "These people are tricking me. They know it's almost twelve. It's good they told me so I can prepare. I will run fast because I don't know if I'll catch that plane... If I don't make it, in any case, I will have to run because of what awaits me with the people there."

"Hey! Hey! Kid! Can't you hear?" they shouted at me as they opened the car door. "Get off here! This avenue takes you right to the entrance of the airport. Remember that if you arrive a minute late, they won't let you in."

I got off and started running. I knew it was already late, the plane was probably taking off. There were many people on the sides forming a barrier. When I passed, they shouted at me loudly: "TRAITOR! SCUM! TRAITOR! SCUM! YOU SOLD US FOR OTHERS WHO AREN'T WORTH IT!"

Almost at the airport, others told me:

GET OUT, BECAUSE IF YOU COME BACK
WE WILL KILL YOU FOR TRAITOR!

I heard everything but ignored it. I continued towards the door and entered. Inside, everything was calm.

"Where are you going?" they asked me as I was heading to the counter.

"I'm going to catch the plane to Spain. They told me it leaves at twelve," I replied very agitated. "If you want to check the list, my name must be there."

"Mmmh, let me see," a man said while checking a paper at the counter. "Indeed, your name is here. Only the plane has already left. Now you have to wait at home until the next appointment. Wait until they notify you again."

I felt completely frustrated. The police intentionally came late for me so I wouldn't catch the flight. And I had to forcefully return through where all those people were, and they were going to hit me. I prepared myself and ran as fast as my legs would go. They started hitting and kicking me all over my body. I tried to defend myself, but there were too many people. They knocked out two molars, and one knee was very swollen, they opened my head. I ran desperately. Suddenly, I heard someone calling me by my name.

"Rolando! Run, kid! Come! Come quickly! Before they catch you! They are behind you!"

I turned to the side and saw a bus stopped there with the door open. The driver was a man who knew me, a friend of my stepfather. Seeing him, I ran up and thanked him infinitely for saving my life. Thanks to him, I made it to my house.

The next day, the neighbors, along with those friends I grew up and played with, came to my house. They caused a scene. They shouted at me with much hatred.

"LET THE SCUM GO! LET THE SCUM GO!"

My sisters, when they heard them shouting, climbed onto the roof of the house. With sticks, stones, hot water, and everything they had at hand, they were ready to defend me.

I wanted to go out, but my mother didn't let me. She went out with a machete and stood right at the gate of the house.

“If you are communists and give your life for communism,” he shouted with great courage, “then I give my life for my son. So leave him alone, because you know he hasn’t done anything to any of you. Now, if you want him, then come for him, because with this machete I will defend him to the end. And one by one you will go with me. If I die, I will do so with great pride, because no one is going to touch my son.”

“Don’t you dare go near my mother! Because if you do, you’ll see what happens,” my sisters shouted from above. When the neighbors saw that they were willing to do anything, they left. They went to the house of a boy who lived a block down from mine. He was also leaving the country. And that’s how they broke the windows. They threw eggs at the house, and several other things.

That boy had to pretend to be homosexual. That was the only way he found to be allowed to leave Cuba. Because Fidel Castro didn't want homosexuals, or criminals, or mentally disabled people, or invalids, or those who spoke badly of the government (usually political prisoners, and some who luckily weren't in prison).

The police went to the houses of all those people and told them they had to leave the country. Without any reason or motive, they forced them. Even when they didn't want to, they were taken against their will.

Three policemen came to my house and knocked on the door. Three days had passed since the last beating. My sister jumped to open the door.

"We are looking for Rolando Castillo. Does he live here?" one of the policemen asked my sister.

"Yes, he lives here. He is my brother. Why do you want him?" she replied.

"We are here for him because he has to leave the country. We hope he is ready because we don't have much time. So tell him to hurry up and no goodbyes."

"But you can't treat my brother like this. He is not a criminal, he is not a delinquent."

"Look miss, call your brother and shut your mouth. If you don't want us to take you to jail."

"Why?"

"Because even if you are his sister and want to defend him, we will not have any consideration. Your brother, in case you don't know, is more than a criminal. He is a TRAITOR TO THE HOMELAND!"

"That is not being a traitor just because he is leaving the country."

"Shut up! We already told you to shut up. And he is a traitor just because he is leaving the country."

"Mmmh, and they say Cuba is free and sovereign? If you can't speak or express yourself, why do they already want to put someone in jail? That is why I wish my brother well and that he has much luck and happiness. I hope he leaves."

"You don't know what you're saying, but fine, wish him all that. You don't know if he will come out of this alive." the policemen told my sister laughing sarcastically.

I was listening to everything my sister spoke with the policemen. I know she did it to give me time to get dressed and leave.

"Don't worry about anything. We have a lot of faith in you and we know you'll do well." my sister told me when I came out. "Walk carefully, because this doesn't sound good."

That day, they put me in their car and took me to José Martí airport. According to what they said, they were going to send me to Peru.

That day I couldn't even get there. People were forming their usual line, and we had to pass through in the middle. They beat us so much that many people died right there. They already left me in very bad shape, opened my head in three different places, fractured a finger. My ankle was very swollen. I couldn't walk. I don't know how I got home alive for the second time.

When my mother saw me, she burst into tears. That hurt me a lot and, even though I didn't want to cry, I did.

"Ronaldito! Look how you've come!", my mother told me crying. "You have to leave those problems, son. Listen to me! One day you won't come home alive."

"Don't worry mom," I replied trying to console her. "Look, this will pass. But please, don't cry."

"Come son, I'll put sugar on your head wounds to stop the bleeding. Look at you. Do you think I am going to be calm? You are losing a lot of blood and I can't take you to the hospital."

"Don't worry. I know I'm not going to the hospital, because they won't treat me. Besides, if people see me again, they'll hit me. I don't want to go through that anymore."

I came to think that the government had given each of us a mark so that wherever they saw us, they would make life impossible for us. I wondered: how much would they pay them to do this to us? And also, if we changed our mind and stayed in Cuba, surely afterward they would kill us themselves.

During those days I was in recovery, I thought about going to the house of a lady who read cards. That is a custom in my country, because since there are no churches people take it as a religion.

"Mom? Can you give me a peso and five cents?" I said to her. "What do you want them for?"

"I want to go with Chucho to have my fortune read."

"Alright," she said while taking out the money.

The lady lived four houses away from mine. I arrived and knocked on the door.

“Boy!” she said, very surprised. “What are you doing in this place? Look at how people are. You have to be careful.”

"It's because I know you won't hate me like the others. You're going to help me, right?”

“Yes, boy, of course! What am I good for?”

“Look, Chucho (that's the lady's name). I've come for you to read my fortune. I don't want to leave without knowing what my future will be! You know what they're doing to us. Sometimes I feel bad and insecure; all those people hit us, and you know it's very difficult like that.”

“Son, you know I charge. Because I don't have money and what they give me is to buy the food I need.”

“Yes, I know. Look, I brought money... How much do you charge to read my fortune?”

“I'm going to charge you a peso and five cents.”

“Alright.”

She took the deck and arranged it on the table.

“Look, son. The cards say that you will travel to the United States. You're going to have a lot of problems, but if you face them, in time you will succeed and have money.”

We spent almost two hours and she explained everything to me step by step. We finished and I decided to go back home.

“Chucho, can I ask you a favor?”

“Tell me, son. What favor?”

“Can you look out onto the street and tell me how things are?”

“Yes, of course.”

She went to look and then came back very distressed. “Ronaldito! Don’t go out. At Hugo's house, they’re causing a big commotion,” she told me. “They’re throwing eggs, stones, and shouting loudly: GET OUT, WE DON’T WANT YOU! GET OUT, WE DON’T WANT YOU!”

“Chucho, can you do me another favor?”

“Yes, tell me.

“I would like you to go to my house and tell my sisters and my brother that I am here at your house. Tell them to get ready because I am going to run to my house.” The lady left and when she returned, I said goodbye to her. "Ronaldito! Don't leave! It's ugly out there in the street! Wait until everything calms down."

"No, no, Chucho. Don't worry. I'm leaving because I don't want to get into trouble."

I ran towards my house. My sisters and brother were already coming for me with sticks and stones. One of my sisters was carrying a bucket with hot water. They were already reaching Chucho's house, and other people were coming up behind them. I tried to warn them, but they didn't hear me. They only saw the people coming towards them. I was in the middle.

I wanted to run, and the people followed me. I had no choice but to face them. They gave me a terrible beating. They opened my head again. They injured my arm with a knife. Three boys I grew up with were hitting me. I was bleeding a lot from my hand. My sister, when she saw that I was fighting with those boys, threw the boiling water at them. She burned some people. I saw that one of those people had half of their body without skin. Seeing that my family was defending me bravely, they opted to withdraw. I thought they would leave me alone at least until I got home. At that moment, I don't know where more people came from, and I ran through all the streets near my house so they wouldn't kill me. Some police officers and the boys who hit me followed. From a distance, I saw an open gate and went in. In the yard, there were four avocado trees. Desperate, I climbed one of them. I didn't think that the avocado branches were very thin and could break at any moment. I climbed to the highest branch. After two minutes, the police and the boys passed by and searched for twenty minutes. They didn't notice me above and opted to leave.

The avocado branches were breaking. I was tired of being up there. I was bleeding a lot from my head and hand. The branch I was on broke, and I slid so quickly down the trunk of the tree that I scraped all my legs. I fell sitting on the ground so hard that I lost my voice. I stood up and made sure there was no one outside. Then, I ran towards the estate behind Rey and Mayito's house. I took a break, but the owner's dog approached me. I thought it was going to bite me, and I got up to jump a wall about eight feet high. I kept jumping through the yards of several houses until I reached my house, all bloody but alive.

"Where is my mom?" I asked my sisters.

"We're so glad you arrived! We thought they had caught you and done something to you! Mom got so nervous that she had a nervous attack and they took her to the hospital!"

"I'm going to my room," I said, worried about my mother. At night, my mother arrived home. She headed to my bedroom. I heard the door open. I was covered up to my head. The light was off. My mother uncovered me and screamed when she saw me.

"Why didn't you say you were like this?" she said to me. "So your sisters could heal you!"

"I didn't say anything because, as you can see, they're lazy," I replied. "And you were in the hospital."

My mother cried as she was healing me. I didn't know how to console her so she wouldn't worry.

"Son, I'm so sorry for everything that's happening," she told me. "But I'm very proud of you. Because you're so strong, and children like you always achieve their goals. Although I know that the day you leave, I'll lose you forever. I love you very much, and I'll never forget you."

We cried together, and then she made me get up and go to the bathroom. She cleaned my wounds with soap. I realized she was still crying.

"What's wrong, mama?" I asked her.

"It's just that I don't want to lose you," she replied very sadly. "I saw what they did to Rey and Mayito. I don't want these communists to do the same to you, son."

"Look," I replied, trying to ease her worries. "You've been the one who has given me the strength to keep going and achieve what I want. If you cry, I suffer a lot. I know you will suffer like me when I leave. That's why right now, all I want is to see you calm. Remember, you've told me that to achieve what one desires, it costs a lot, and that price must be paid. I want you by my side just like now, with that courage and bravery, and don't worry or cry."

That day, I really didn't want my sisters or the woman I had to see me. I was living with a young woman who was already five months pregnant. If she had seen me like that, she would have had a miscarriage. My nerves were completely on edge to the point that when I heard a noise, I thought it was people wanting to hit me, so I punched the air. My mom was the only one who came to check on me. When she did, I tried to hit her, but she slapped me to make me react.

Alone, I thought: How is it possible that the people I've known since I was a child and my friends, who I played with so many times, want to kill me? All because they blindly believe in communism. Don't they remember that as children we all dreamed?

"I would like," one would say, "my dad to buy me a bicycle."

"I want," another would say, "a fire truck."

"I want an ambulance." We all asked for more or less the same because each of us wanted something. We lived on dreams.

That was one of the reasons why I cried.

My mom, when she got home from work, would heal my wounds. I was like that for three days.

5
PORT OF MARIEL

It was eleven in the morning on the fourth day. It was very hot. In the blue sky, a flock of seagulls flew by. The trees swayed gently. Some birds sang happily. It occurred to me to go to the store in front of my house. I was chatting with the owners of the place.

"Ronaldito, it's good that you're leaving here!" they said to me. "We hope everything goes well for you! And we wish you the best of luck!"

"Thank you. I hope to leave soon," I replied.

"Don't you know when you're leaving?"

"No. They promised to let me know. I still don't know when I'll leave."

In the distance, I saw a car approaching; it was from the State. I immediately headed to my house.

"Does Rolando Castillo live here?" they asked me when I was opening the gate to my house.

"Yes. That's me," I replied a bit distrustfully, given what had happened to me before.

"Well then. You have five minutes to get dressed because you're coming with us."

"Okay. I'll go get dressed," I told them as I went into the house to put on pants and a shirt because I had a t-shirt and shorts on due to the heat that day.

I entered my room very hurriedly. I looked for my clothes and immediately put them on. My mom was working. I didn't know what to do because I wanted to say goodbye to her before leaving. The officers were waiting in the car, and my sister and the woman I was with saw that I was nervous.

"Who are those men?" they asked me curiously.

"Those men came to get me to kick me out of the country."

"What? Are you leaving already?" they said and started crying.

"Don't cry or worry," I replied. "I'll be fine! Tell Mimi (that's what I called my mother) that I'll call her as soon as I have a chance."

"Take good care of yourself and don't let anyone fool you," my woman told me with tears in her eyes. "Because remember, they've already hurt you a lot. So stay sharp..."

He did not continue speaking because the words got stuck in his throat. "Don't worry, if I achieve what I want, I will send for you," I replied, trying to encourage them.

My brother arrived just as I was going out to the street.

"Rolando, I want to go with you. Please take me!"

"No, Pedrito! The men waiting will not take you. But as soon as I settle down," I replied to calm him, "I will send for you."

The guards who were waiting hurried me and took my brother aside.

"You're not going, right?"

"That's what I'm telling my brother, to see if he takes me with him."

The guards pushed him, put handcuffs on me, and shoved me into the car.

"Now you're in our custody," they told me. "Don't try to do anything and everything will go smoothly. But if you do something, you won't be able to leave the country. Besides, you will regret it."

I remained very calm and since I had the handcuffs, I couldn't defend myself. So I had to do what they wanted. They took me to a place they had prepared. They called it "four wheels." I don't know why they called it that. I was surprised to see so many people who also wanted to leave. They removed my handcuffs and left me in there. Then I truly believed I was leaving Cuba. That night we slept like animals. All on the floor and without covering ourselves. But peacefully! The place was small. I stayed there for three days. Every day five buses would arrive, filled with those of us who were there. The police were patrolling around.

On the second day, buses arrived and they started calling people by their names. They had our names written on lists. I realized they had us well controlled. To board the bus, they put them in lines. That was the method they used to prevent people outside from sneaking in. Because the day before, some had done so. I heard several screams and turned to see what was happening. I saw that about two hundred people were approaching. The closer they came, the better I could hear what they were shouting.

"LET THEM GO! WE DON'T WANT SCUM HERE!"

Seeing so many people, I thought we would get beaten again. So I looked for a corner to be safer. I was still sore from the beating I received in previous days. People were yelling at us, and I was terrified, seeing their faces full of hatred. They approached us, and the guards were prepared. They feared another uproar. Suddenly, about ten people, both men and women, emerged from among the shouting crowd. They tried to get to where we were. I watched everything from a distance and heard gunshots. Minutes later, I saw ambulances coming and going. It seemed they were carrying several injured people by the same police. In that chaos, five people managed to get in, and then the people inside beat them and expelled them from there. The roles had been reversed. The police immediately handcuffed them and took them away.

I imagine they felt the same as we did when they humiliated and beat us.

That day I didn't sleep anymore; I distrusted even my own shadow. The third day in the morning, it was cool; the sun wasn't shining brightly yet. The buses arrived, and the guards started calling names. I was among the first to be called. I approached a table where a very dark-skinned man with a foul smell was giving a number.

"Take this number, scum," the man said to me. "Tell us why you want to leave the country!"

"Why are you asking me? If you already know why!" I replied somewhat violently.

"I asked why you want to leave the country, unhappy black man!"

"I come from the Peruvian Embassy," I replied, annoyed by the way he addressed me. "Now you know why I want to leave."

"They heard! This is one of the ones who started this revolt!" I shouted to his colleagues loudly so they could hear. The guards turned to look at me.

"That's one of the ones who got into the Embassy," shouted another guard, pointing at me. "And because of him, we have to pay!"

The people who were standing in line with me started to applaud. And from there others followed. I felt like a hero. The guards did not expect such a reaction. They were stunned. They forgot they were interrogating me. Outside, people went silent, wanting to find out why there was applause inside. I headed towards the bus I was assigned to. I boarded the vehicle, and the people there shook my hand and applauded too.

In the three days I spent in the "four wheels," I observed that several people from outside dressed up as homosexuals to be allowed to leave the country. Others pretended to be crazy. And the wives of prisoners also came with their children to say they wouldn't leave their husbands alone.

The bus started heading towards the Port of Mariel. The people who were with me began to ask me questions.

"Boy! How is it that you are alive? How did you manage to get here?"

"I don't even want to remember," I told them. "But we know you had it bad," others said. "Because most of those who were at the Embassy were killed. Isn't it true that they were sent to other countries?"

"Well, I don't know what happened to them," I would say so they wouldn't keep asking, because I no longer trusted anyone. "The important thing is that those of us who are in this now have the strength to move forward until we are given freedom."

They also asked me questions about how the situation was at the Embassy and how many days I spent stuck in that place. I didn't want to say anything because of the guards who were with us, making sure no one got on and monitoring that everyone was in their place, since the prisoners only had a number and I was the only one with a safe-conduct, passport, and visa.

We traveled for two hours. They kept insisting for me to tell them about the Embassy. I was eager to reach Mariel to avoid all those questions. Finally, we arrived. We got off the bus and formed two lines, then walked down a sandy path towards the tented sections on the beach.

"Scum! We've arrived at Mariel!" said a guard in an arrogant tone. "Get off in order! Men, make a line on the right side! Women with children on the left side!" We lined up as we were instructed. The women with the children were the wives and children of the prisoners.

"Pay attention," they told us through a loudspeaker. "Those who have watches, chains, photos, money, and other metallic items, you have to take them off to pass through the metal detector. If you don't, we will strip you of all your clothes and check you up to your ears! In this country, you have to leave everything! There are envelopes on that table," they said pointing ahead. "Put your things there, and we will send them to your relatives or the address you provide."

That day we were searched. The women were taken to one section and the men to another. They made us strip and searched us thoroughly to make sure we weren't hiding anything. I put all the things I carried, like photos, wallet, ID card, ring, etc., in an envelope to which I wrote my home address.

Later I found out that they kept everything that suited them. What they didn't like, they threw away or burned. At least my family didn't receive anything.

I went through the detector and from there we were taken to very large tents. They said that each of the tents was a section. So they separated all of us: in one were the criminals, in another the mentally ill with disabilities, in the next were homosexuals with criminal records, in another political prisoners or those who disagreed with the government system, and in the last were all of us from the Embassy, of which there were very few. I wanted to investigate to see what was happening and walked inside.

"Look, boy, stay in your place if you want to leave the country," one of the guards told me. "All right," I replied, returning to my section.

From where I was, I saw many private ships. I thought the owners were looking for their loved ones, but that was not the case. They offered their ship just so they could leave with their family. Inside the place, it was as if we were in Hitler's times, because all the guards watching us had German shepherd dogs.

That day I saw buses full of prisoners handcuffed hands and feet arriving. There was a lot of security, although some guards did not do their job. One of them was talking to a very good-looking girl when a problem arose among the prisoners. The guard forgot about the dog and ran to see what was happening.

A few steps from the animal was a five or six-year-old boy playing. The dog went towards the little boy and bit him, tearing a piece of his leg. Then, the dog lay down and started eating the child's flesh. I tried to approach the animal, but the boy's mother got ahead of me. However, the dog also attacked her, causing several bites. When the guard returned, he did nothing.

"Look, ma'am!" the guard told the woman. "I left the dog tied up, it was because your son came to bother him. And if you tried to hit him, the animal only defended himself."

That was the biggest lie I had ever heard in my life.

It was one in the afternoon when they called me to join the lineup with other people, as we were going to be taken to the ship assigned to us. Many people were crying because they didn't want to leave the country, but Fidel didn't care about that. They were forced to leave just for speaking ill of the government or because they had physical deficiencies. In the line where I stood, some women with their children were formed. The vast majority were prisoners. The guard directed us towards the ship.

"Scum! Let me see how many people I can fit in this boat," the guard told us, moving away.

He returned and gave the order for us to board the ship. I was one of the first to get on and quickly headed to the bow of the ship.

I stayed watching everything that was happening and saw the owner of the boat come out.

"Officer, only eighty people can board this boat. This is a shrimp boat!" said the owner.

"In this shrimp boat," replied the guard somewhat annoyed, "three hundred and fifty people have to leave. Afterward, we'll let you take your family."

The man might have been nervous about what the guard had said and took out a candy to eat. Then he threw the wrapper into the water.

"You know something," said the guard upon seeing him throw the paper. "Now you have to pay five hundred dollars for throwing the little paper, just like because the government's laws are like that."

"No, you're crazy. As far as I know, no one is fined for throwing a paper. No one that I understand," responded the man.

"I'm just following orders, and if you don't want to pay the fine, you won't move from here, even if we brought your family. So pay, because this is Cuba, whether you like it or not."

The owner of the boat had no other choice but to pay the fine demanded by the guard. The man was very upset because the money he paid was needed so his family wouldn't go hungry in the country where we were going to arrive.

6

THE GOODBYE

The news of that day predicted bad weather for the night. I didn't worry, thinking that once all the people boarded the ship, we would leave. But it wasn't like that. Once the small boats were full, they were directed to the opposite side from where the empty ones were. There, they had to wait for the other boats to fill up. They let them go out in groups. They exploited the owners because once the boat was ready to set sail, they made the owner responsible for the entire vessel. There were very small boats approximately twenty-four feet long. In those little boats, they packed one hundred to one hundred and fifty people. Mr. Fidel didn't care about that; the only thing he wanted was to get rid of the "scum," as they called us.

I was very worried about passing through the Bermuda Triangle. I frequently heard comments about ships and planes disappearing without a trace when passing through that place. While thinking about surviving wherever luck would take us, I fell asleep.

"Get ready! Because in a few minutes you will be able to leave!" the guard told the people. Everyone started shouting:

"Freedom, freedom!"

I woke up a little dazed, not knowing why people were shouting. A man told me that we were leaving. It was about six in the evening, and the sea was already starting to get choppy. Minutes later, some guards approached in a small motorboat and through a speaker said that we could leave. I looked up and saw the dark sky, the clouds moving rapidly. But those communists didn't care. I'm sure they thought that if we wanted to leave, we had to pass the last and most difficult test: the struggle for life to be as free as the wind.

The ship started moving. I saw the shore of the beach and thought: "My life from this moment will change, and I will be born again. Without a mother, without siblings... alone. Is my mom around at this moment? When will I set foot in my country again? Is my family remembering me?" The ship moved away, and I kept my eyes fixed on the beach shore. I wanted to hold back the urge to cry so no one would see me. A woman approached and saw me with tears in my eyes.

"Do you want me to help you let it out, boy?" she said to me.

I turned to look at her.

"Look! Look at your country for the last time!" the lady told me, crying. "Because who knows if we'll ever see it again. I also left my children and grandchildren, all my family whom I love so much. But in this country, it isn't easy to seek freedom, where the communists live well. Here there is no freedom of expression, there is no religion, and in the end, they do what the government wants."

"Yes, it's true," I replied. "I was told that in the United States when people arrive who are not from that country, they unleash the dogs on them. Castro himself has said so. I was also told that they are very racist there and if they see a black person, they also punish them by unleashing the dogs. I want to show the world that my country is a hell. Not everyone knows it. I feel sad and also full of hatred towards Castro, because because of him I have to leave this beautiful country."

"In this country, not even the animals are happy," the lady told me. "Do you know why? Because many times we have to hunt them to eat! What the government provides is not enough for us to eat throughout the month. It's true, many times I fell asleep with an empty stomach and the next day I had to go to school. While Fidel and his brother Raul slept with full stomachs, we had to figure out how to get food after school."

"Wherever we get to," the lady told me, "you will try some fruits that we don't have here. They are called grapes, apples, pears, strawberries. Have you ever eaten them?"

"Oh, yes, I only ate grapes, apples, and pears once, not the others," I replied.

"Well, Fidel also banned us from eating even those," the lady said angrily. "And believe it or not, they also celebrate Christmas. But the communist people don't know about it!"

"Yes, for sure. They have their eyes closed."

That afternoon the lady and I cried. We watched as we moved away from our land. I felt an infinite sadness. I was thoughtful. "I wonder how my poor mother is now, with the loss of a son? My sisters stayed crying and my brother wanted to come with me. But what would my mother have done if both of us were here? She is, my mother, thinking of me, thinking that maybe I won't return. Thinking that I love my family so much, with all my heart. My brother is going to need me as much as I need him, and it's only because of the government system that we have to leave our country. Our family is forced to do so. I hate Fidel! I hate Raul! I hate their system! Free seeing that I was moving away from my country. I cried seeing that this beloved land was slipping from my hands. I felt as if a part of me was dying. With the movement of the boat and thinking about what I wanted, I fell asleep. A wave hit the boat very hard and woke me up. I crouched and stood up again. I saw an enormous wave coming towards where I was. The boat almost sank!"

"My God!", I said. "Help me in this situation! It's the first time I see something like this."

I crouched and felt how the boat went up and down. There were so many people on the boat that it was too heavy. Between the edge of the boat and the water, there was only one foot of distance or less.

"Excuse me, sir," I asked a man who was near me, "have we been sailing for a long time?"

"Yes, boy. We've been sailing for two hours or more," the man replied. "You came asleep, right?"

"Yes, it's because I was tired. You know! So many days without sleep," I told him.

The sea was completely furious. The captain of the boat presented himself to us.

"Ladies and gentlemen! I am the owner of the boat and the captain of this journey. I feel very happy because, in exchange for having all of you with me, even though there are many of you, I could recover what I lost for more than twenty years. I was imprisoned for political reasons, and the most important thing is that my family is with me. Thanks to all of you! We're going to have a tough time because a storm is coming. If you listen to what I say, everything will turn out fine. Don't drink water because you might throw up!"

7
THE TRAGEDY

"Ma'am, excuse me. Do you know what time it is?" I asked a lady who was near me again. I wasn't very sure about what the previous man had told me about the time.

"Maybe eight at night," she told me. "It's been more than two hours since we left Mariel."

More than two hours had passed, but I thought I had only slept for ten minutes.

"Thank you. I heard someone shouting," I told her.

"Yes, but maybe it's the wind," she replied. "With this bad weather, sometimes the air whistles."

I heard someone shouting in the distance, but it didn't occur to me to look. I crawled to the place where I had settled when I got on the boat. I felt dizzy. Again, I heard screams.

I looked out and didn't see all the boats that left with us. I observed closely and some were missing. In reality, the missing ones were the small boats. I imagined they had sunk. The sea was so furious that when the waves rose, they lifted the boats more than ten feet. I sat down because I got very dizzy. I heard many screams in the distance. I tried to pay attention to listen better and I managed to hear what they were saying.

"Help me! Please!" they were shouting.

"Don't move!" someone was saying.

"Hold on there and don't let go!"

I got up to see what was happening. The lights from the shrimp boats illuminated, and then I saw that two small boats disappeared, and people were screaming desperately when they realized they couldn't do anything for those who were lost at sea. I remember that nothing was left of those two small boats. They disappeared with everything and everyone. It all happened so quickly that I couldn't believe it. Then I remembered that in Cuba, several times I heard about mysterious disappearances in the Bermuda Triangle. That day, with the impression of seeing how a third boat disappeared, I related those tragedies to the Triangle disappearances.

"Comrade, did you see what just happened to those boats?" commented two people in front of me.

"Yes, sir, I saw it, and I still can't believe it," replied the other. "Maybe we are going through the Triangle, and we haven't realized it," commented a third person. "Because there was not a trace of the people! Those boats sank from the weight they were carrying."

"I'm not saying, of course they sank. The people who saw what happened to those boats could never have imagined what we were going to see next.

"Ladies and gentlemen! Pay attention!" shouted the captain of the boat I was on. "Move toward the center of the boat as much as you can and hold onto each other. It's to keep the boat leveled."

I kept an eye on the little boats that were with us. There was one that measured about twenty-one to twenty-two feet long and had around one hundred and fifty people on board. What recklessness of Fidel, he gave the order for the boats to be filled beyond their capacity!

About forty minutes passed. Again, several screams were heard. I got up to see what was happening, and what I saw left me terrified. I no longer saw the boats I had seen earlier. There were sharks attacking the people from a sunken boat. I don't know how many sharks there were. All I saw were the animals' fins. The poor people were screaming for help. The sharks were having a macabre feast, pulling people. I looked around, and there came a boat with about fifty people following us to the Gulf of Mexico, and then I didn't see it anymore. Almost at our level was a boat that maybe measured twenty-two feet and had many people, far beyond its capacity. And reaching the Gulf, it split in half, along with another that seemed to be following it. The people fell into the sea, screaming desperately. I felt powerless because I couldn't do anything. Many people were holding onto empty oil barrels. When the lights from the boats illuminated the tragic scene, I saw how the sharks were pulling people.

The water there was full of oil. Many people were burning because of that liquid and the saltwater. The weather was very bad. Lightning could be seen in the sky in the distance, the wind was blowing stronger, and the waves were rising higher, about twelve feet high.

The captain told us that this was a current zone and that he could not stop.

"Ladies and gentlemen! I would like to help those poor people who are dying, but here," said the captain of the boat, "I cannot stop because the currents are very dangerous, and we could overturn. Also, with the weight of the ship, we would sink."

Some boats could no longer continue and stopped halfway. They were sinking. The captain only managed to tow one of them that was about twenty-two or twenty-three feet long.

"May God protect them!" said a lady. "Since we cannot help them. Too many people have already been lost."

"Yes, it's true," replied a man. "I saw not long ago how a shark ate a person. And even children fell into the water."

"Help us! Please, help us!" shouted a man in the middle of the boat. "This lady passed out! I think it was from the fright of seeing how the sharks were wiping out people."

One lady and another man approached to help some people who suffered a nervous attack.

"Look, ma'am, put this piece of cloth," said a man to the woman who approached to help, "I've already wet it! Put it on her head to cool her down, that lady."

Everything happened so quickly that in the minutes I was observing, I felt completely desperate, seeing the poor people who only screamed once and then sank. And all that was visible were many shark fins.

Half an hour later, two helicopters with very large lights passed over us. Upon observing them closely, I realized they were from the Red Cross. Later, I learned that they helped all the people floating, holding onto the already empty oil barrels. They transported them in those helicopters to Key West. Those people arrived almost without skin, as the saltwater with the oil had burned them.

"Thank you, my God, for sending help!" said an old lady. "At least the Red Cross will help them. I hope everyone was saved so they can enjoy freedom."

With the bad weather and the misfortune of those people, we had been sailing for almost ten hours. I heard some of those on the boat shouting. I quickly got up.

"Comrades! Look! Look over there! You can see lights!" said someone. "We're already getting to somewhere!"

"It's true, there are lights," shouted someone else.

"My God, thank you!" said some ladies. "For helping us get out of this situation alive."

"See those lights in the distance," the captain told us. "That's Key West. We're reaching the United States, which means we're safe."

I got up and kept staring. I saw the lights so far away that I felt great despair. I wanted to be there. It was as if I started living again.

"How do they live in that country? If the communists hadn't taken away the addresses my mother gave me, I would have gone to one of those houses once I got there. Being there, where will I stay? Maybe they'll give us a place to live while we look for somewhere to stay. If it weren't the United States, what country would we have reached?"

He had told me: "Yes, boy, in the United States you live well," said my stepfather. "It's not like here. There you eat what you want and live how you want. They pay you well at any job."

"I would like to go," I told him. "But how do I leave this country?"

"You'll have the opportunity. And when it comes, take advantage of it!"

"But Castro says in his speeches that in that country they set the dogs on you when you're not from there. Especially if you're black."

"Who do you listen to? I already told you it's different. There you're free."

"I'm going to find a way to leave," I replied pensively. I always tried to invent something but it never worked. Now that I'm here, I have to take advantage of this opportunity."

8

KEY WEST

When we arrived at the port of Key West, it was around five in the morning. There was a small boat with some guards on board who told us we had to wait until they finished with the other ships that arrived first. We stayed in that place for about three hours. I wanted to find out what the officers had said. Why were they making us wait so long? I was too hungry and couldn't take it anymore. The owner of the boat explained to us why we had to wait. It was to check the documents of the people who arrived before us.

At eight in the morning, the boat returned with four naval officers, telling the captain to bring the ship closer to the shore and to disembark slowly in a line so that everything would be smooth and quick.

We started disembarking in line, and further ahead many Immigration people were waiting for us.

When it was my turn, I went to the first Immigration desk. I was a little nervous due to hunger and fatigue. I remembered again that sometimes Fidel Castro told us that in the United States foreign people were awaited with dogs, even more so if we were black because they had a lot of hatred for people of color.

I stood in front of two officers sitting at the table. I was nervous because I didn't know how to speak English.

Those words that they said in Cuba came to me again: "And when you get to that country, they will be waiting for you with dogs." I was amazed because it was the complete opposite; they were treating us very well. Everything they told us in my country was a lie.

"Young man! Hey!" said the guard. "Are you okay?"

However, I felt great relief when I heard that guard speak to me in Spanish.

"Huh? Oh, sorry, I didn't hear you," I said.

"Yes, I noticed that you are very thoughtful, or maybe amazed, right?"

"Yes, it's amazement," I replied.

"We thought you didn't speak, that you were deaf-mute," the officer told me. "I called you three times and you didn't hear me."

"Excuse me, sir, but I was a little distracted," I replied.

"Look, we want to ask you something. Why are you the only one who has a passport, visa, and a safe-conduct?" the officer asked me.

"Why are you asking me that, sir?" I replied a little puzzled, as I thought that was a problem.

"Because all the people who came on the boat you traveled on have no papers, and you are the only one who came with enough documents to enter this country."

"Is that true?" I asked, a little more confident.

"Yes, it's true," he replied, "I asked you because everyone else came with a number which also has the names of the family members they traveled with. Do you understand me, boy?"

"Yes, I understand you," I said, "it's just surprising to me that I'm the only one with papers, I thought there were more with me."

"Well, look, only you are in that situation."

"Ah, I see!" I replied.

"Look, what I want to tell you is this," he told me again, "how did you get these papers? Because other people don't have them."

"I received them days before leaving Mariel," I replied. When I said that, the gentleman signaled to another officer who immediately approached.

"Come with me, I'll take care of you," said the other officer.

I got up and followed him. He led me to a small room near the table where I was interviewed. The officer opened the door.

"Come in and sit down," he said to me.

I sat down and saw that the man took out a notebook in which he had something written.

"Now, answer the questions I'm going to ask you," he said.

"Alright, Sir," I replied.

"What's your name?" he asked me.

"My name is Rolando Castillo," I said in a tone of mistrust.

"Were you in the Cuban Army?" he continued asking.

"Yes," I said. "In the Youth Army. There I studied and worked."

"And how was it that, if you were studying and working, you wanted to come to this country?" he said a bit doubtful, "without having family or knowing anyone."

"I came to this country because I know I'm young and I think that here I'll have the opportunity to help my family. To work in a place where I can benefit. To not live deprived of many things that in my country I can't obtain. Because they exist, but we don't have the opportunity to acquire them."

"What things are you referring to?" he asked somewhat intrigued.

"For example, clothes. Now I will be able to buy clothes to my liking. Eat all I want. Wear shoes as I wish. In other words, live to my liking. And this is an opportunity I want to take advantage of."

"And do you think you'll do all that you've told me?" he asked somewhat curious.

"Yes, yes I will. Because I know I have been reborn."

After listening to me with great attention, the man gave me some papers to sign. Once I signed them, he gave me a work permit and a paper called I-94, which is a migration document.

"Look, kid, that's all," he said. "You can now go eat something. It looks like you're really hungry."

"Alright. Thank you, sir," I said full of joy.

"Oh! Look, we don't know how long you'll be here in these tents," he said. "But we will relocate you very soon. And in the other place you'll stay until a sponsor appears who wants to be your guardian. To make sure you will have a house and a job."

"Alright, officer. I thank you very much," I said with more enthusiasm. With a tremendous smile, I headed to the dining hall.

When I entered that place, I stopped suddenly. I had never seen so much food. Also, it had been more than sixteen years since I'd seen apples by the bunch, like I was seeing them at that moment. I turned my face and saw grapes! Of two or three kinds! And many more things. For me, it was incredible. I gathered myself and kept walking. When I arrived, I didn't know where to start. I took several foods and sat down. A guard arrived and told us:

"You have already achieved what you wanted. Now, the only thing I ask is that you pray for this plate of food that God has given you and then you can eat all you want. When you finish, I will guide you to where your waiting camp is."

That day I ate a bit of everything. I felt very happy. But soon after, I started with a terrible stomach ache. All because it had been many years since I had eaten that way. I got chills and started to vomit.

"What's happening to you, boy?" a guard asked me.

"It's just that I hadn't eaten like this for a long time! But I'll get over it quickly. Thank you, sir!"

That day, after that discomfort, I decided to wait a while and went back to the dining hall. But now with the previous experience, I didn't eat as much.

After finishing, the guard pointed out where the dormitories were, which were large tents with beds arranged in rows.

About twenty feet away was the sea. In itself, the place was very nice. I was eager to get out of there and to know more beyond. I stayed there for two and a half days.

"Come closer, boy," the guard said to me. "You will stay in this house. They will come to find you later."

"Will I be here for a long time?" I asked him.

"It all depends on when your name appears on the officials' lists," he said to me, "and that depends on whether they have a place for you."

"Won't I stay here until I find a place to live?"

"No. Look, since you're underage, they will find a person or a family to sponsor you," he told me. "Someone to take responsibility for you. Meanwhile, you will live under government care. But not here. As I said, in another place, because this is not a permanent camp."

"Alright. I'll wait."

The guard left and I entered the house. Inside, several gentlemen were chatting. I approached to greet them.

"Good afternoon," I said.

They all answered me at the same time.

"What's your name, boy?" a gentleman asked me.

"My name is Rolando Castillo."

"When did you arrive in this country?" another asked.

"Today at five in the morning," I replied.

"Why did they bring you to the camp at this hour?" a young man asked me.

"I don't know. They didn't tell me."

In that house, there were only fifteen of us. That night, I slept like I never had before. The next day, I toured the camp and noticed that there were too many people.

"What's your name, boy?" a prisoner who approached me asked.

"Rolando," I told him.

"When did you come here?"

"I arrived yesterday at five in the morning."

"Were you also thrown out of Cuba?"

"No, I left because I wanted to be free from communism."

"Oh, that's good! Because I wanted to be near my family, and you see how things are. I couldn't achieve it!"

"Yes, I understand how you feel because I came but had to leave my family. I hope to work soon and help my mother and siblings."

"Well, I was imprisoned; I didn't want to come here," said the man. "And here I am, taken out of the country by force. They didn't even ask for my opinion."

"They did the same to me," said another prisoner who approached when he heard our conversation. "I couldn't even talk to my family. They probably don't know about me yet."

"Well, we're in the same situation," answered a third. "They didn't even tell me I had to leave. They just came and cuffed me. I thought they would transfer me to another place, and when I realized it, I was already in Mariel."

"Let's see when we can return to our country," answered a woman. "Because the truth is, Fidel doesn't want us. If we return, they will surely kill us. I left of my own free will. You see how things are, and I need to help my family."

That's how I met many men and women who were forced out by the communists. Others told me that, rather than stay in prison for years in Cuba, they preferred to come since here they would be free.

A girl I met surprised me with her talk.

"What's your name?" I asked a girl who was alone and very sad.

"Leonor. And what's your name?" she asked me.

"My name is Rolando," I told her. "I approached you because you look very sad. Is it because of your family, right? Or are they with you?"

"No. My family stayed in Cuba," she replied. "That's why I feel depressed."

"Why did you come?"

"Because I was imprisoned in Cuba. I had a sentence of several years, and I didn't do much harm to deserve so many years."

"What did you do?"

"Well, it was all because one day a woman offended me, and I got very upset and responded badly to her. After arguing, we fought in the middle of the street. It turns out the woman belonged to the committee. And you know, she sued me, and I was judged for 'violation of communism.' They sentenced me to fifteen years in prison!" I saw the girl began to cry.

"Don't cry. The important thing is that you're here, and you can do things that there, being locked up, you would never do."

"Yes, you're right. But now I cry because I'm very far from my family."

"I understand because I'm in the same position as you. I just left that country, leaving my family behind, because of the political system. You know... communism. I don't like it. I know I will suffer, but... we have to be strong and move forward."

I noticed she listened to me and calmed down. That day, after consoling each other, we said goodbye. Elia went to her dormitory, and I did the same.

The next day in the morning, when they started serving breakfast, those with papers went in first, followed by those who only had a slip of paper.

Several prisoners were having breakfast. Suddenly, two people there began to fight. One had to be urgently taken to the hospital because the other injured him with a knife.

"How can they do such things!" commented a woman who was watching the cruel scene. "They should behave now that they are miraculously free and alive."

"Yes, that's true," I said.

"And do you know why they fought?"

"No, I don't know."

"It's because they already hated each other from Cuba, and they met here. According to a man who knows them told me."

"That's wrong. They should be calmer."

That day, after what happened, everything remained calm. I sat in a place where I could see the sea, which was twenty feet from the camp. The temperature was around eighty degrees. We took a little bath daily. The guards did not allow us to approach the water because it was dangerous to swim in that area. But when they left, we went in to bathe.

The next day, I woke up very early and, after brushing my teeth and washing my face, I went to the dining room for breakfast. I immediately returned to the campsite because between ten and eleven in the morning, buses arrived to take people to the airport and then to shelters. A guard, using a loudspeaker, called people by name, and if the person didn't hear, they went to their dorm to find them.

"Hey, Rolando!" one of my dorm mates said to me. "They've already called you over the loudspeaker! And they have also come to look for you! Go, hurry, you don't want them to leave without you."

Immediately, I headed to where the guards were. I was very happy because I felt everything was getting easier for me.

"Are you Rolando Castillo?" a guard asked me.

"Yes, officer, that's me," I replied immediately.

"Once we've checked your documents, board that bus and wait inside until it fills up, then we'll explain things to you."

They asked for my papers and then I headed towards the bus they had assigned me. It filled up quickly.

"Please, listen!" said a guard who got on the bus. "They will take you to the Key West airport. From there, they will fly you to the Indian People's Camp. You will stay there until they find a sponsor who will take responsibility for you. The agencies willing to help will find work for you until you can decide your own destinies.

"I'm sure you will succeed! I wish you the best of luck!"

We left the camp heading to the airport. I sat next to the window and observed the streets, the houses, the grass, everything seemed very beautiful to me. I don't know if it was because I was already free, but I felt happy. We arrived at the airport and quickly boarded the plane, which then took us to a shelter. Once on the plane, I was assigned a seat next to the window. The officers in charge of the aircraft were very kind. I fastened my seatbelt and shortly after, the plane started to taxi down the runway and took off, gaining stability.

During the flight, I only saw clouds, which relaxed me and made me think that sometimes clouds turn dark, announcing a storm. At those times, the pilot asks the control tower for permission over the radio to climb higher than the clouds and thus fly above the storm, staying out of danger.

My heart felt a series of conflicting emotions. I could sense that after the storm, calm would come, and maybe I could be completely free.

A sensation of chills mixed with a slight fear of the unknown invaded me, but I also felt a surge of hysteria, laughter with tears, for being about to achieve what is most precious to a human being: freedom. Despite these challenging times, I was in search of better days, and at least I was safe. I refused to let anxiety hide my new opportunities. Though life had given me many setbacks, I still had many reasons to seek my freedom at any cost. There were many things I wanted to do, say, give, and share. I just had to fight for my dreams to reach the goal. I needed to maintain the courage to try something new. I couldn't help but feel sadness and nostalgia for my mother and siblings. I missed them so much... When things went wrong, my mother's understanding and strength helped me move forward. Her support and patience always inspired me to do my best.

"I shouldn't worry so much. I think everything is going well. I hope it is. Children like you always achieve their goals. Although I know that the day you leave, I will lose you forever. I love you very much and I will never forget you."

My dear mother! How is she? I wish she could see me and be here so she wouldn't suffer!

"I don't want to lose you... I saw how they left Rey and Mayito. I don't want the same thing to happen to you."

My mother's words came to my mind. I felt very sad and wanted to cry. However, my courage and determination made me see things differently at that moment. I realized I was on the plane heading to an unknown place.

"You have to be strong, Rolando," I told myself. "Think that you're alive and that you have to find a way to help your family. It's a miracle you escaped! That means a lot, it means the opportunity to achieve what you want is just beginning to present itself."

I don't know how long I spent thinking. When I realized it, we had already arrived. The plane was landing. Later, I found out we had flown for two hours. Upon disembarking, several buses were waiting for us, five or six, I don't remember.

Everything was very well organized. After getting off the plane, we boarded different buses: single women, children, families.

The children who went up alone were taken on a bus; they were children who had lost their parents and relatives, just like the women who were alone.

Upon arriving at the shelter, we were settled in the same order. In that place, the houses were long and two stories high. Inside, there were many beds, and I was placed in zone three, house number twenty-three. By chance, there were only twenty-three of us there. The shelter was surrounded by mountains, and the camp was in the middle. It was a beautiful place. Being a military zone, everywhere I looked I saw only officers. Since I arrived at the shelter, I would usually wander around that area just to see if I could find any family members.

"Kid," a dorm mate said to me. "You don’t need to walk around the shelter every day. Look near the offices, there’s a wall where they post lists with the names of those who come and go from here. Go and check it."

"Yes, I didn’t know. I’ll go tomorrow," I replied.

9
THE INDIAN VILLAGE CAMP

I had been wandering around the entire place daily for a month, until a companion told me about the lists. On the second day of reading those sheets, I was heading to the dorm when a man called me.

"Hey! Kid! Don't you know who I am?" the man shouted as he approached me.

"Your face looks familiar," I replied, slightly frowning. "But I don't remember who you are."

"Come with me to the barrack (dormitory) where I am," he said, very cheerfully. "There, I'll tell you who I am, and you'll surely remember me!"

I walked with him to his barrack, remembering it was in zone two, house number twenty-four.

"Sit down and get comfortable, please," he said as he sat next to me and put his right arm over my shoulder. "Look, I am your father's brother. And to assure you of what I say, I'm going to tell you what happened to me. I had a very serious and intense problem that called for my death. As my brother, your father, was a judge at that time... He fought so hard so they wouldn't kill me, that he managed to have me pardoned. In return, he had to sentence me to fifteen years in prison."

"He's still a judge," I replied. "I do remember something about that problem."

"Yes! Do you remember me then?" At that time, I felt very happy because they didn't kill me, but later I got very sad because he sentenced me to fifteen years in prison. And thanks to this opportunity, I am free! But tell me, do you remember me now?"

"Not much. You don't look much like my father," I replied, annoyed. "And you haven't said anything about my mom. I'm sure you knew her. It doesn't matter how bad my father was to you."

"How could I not know your mom!" he replied. "She never agreed with the sentence your father passed on me. And according to Cuban laws, I came out fine. They couldn't release me to the streets after all the harm I caused. That's why your father was forced to give me that sentence."

I was content. What I could never accept is that my own brother sentenced me to so many years, without realizing why I did what I did. I harbor no resentment, and I will not hold any, but I always thought that when I got out, I would go to him to tell him that I suffered too much there because of him. After he told me everything that had happened between him and my father, I confirmed that he was my uncle. He told me some things from when I was a child. I remember that this man was one of my favorite uncles. Since I hadn't seen him for over ten years, I didn't remember him at that moment.

We talked so much that we didn't realize it was already night and time to go to sleep. In that shelter, after ten at night, we all had to be inside the dorms.

"Well, Uncle Gregorio," I said before I was sent to my dormitory, "I'm leaving. I don't want any trouble or to be reprimanded. See you tomorrow!"

"Alright. Go carefully. See you tomorrow!"

Early the next morning, I headed to the bathroom to wash my face and teeth. Then I went to the dining hall, and after finishing my breakfast, I decided to return to my dormitory. At the door, my uncle and three of his friends were waiting for me, but I didn't like them.

"What's wrong, nephew?" my uncle, knowing my demeanor, said to me.

"No, nothing is wrong," I replied in a disdainful tone.

"Come! Let's go over there. We have a lot to talk about," he said, throwing his arm around my shoulder. "Wait a moment! I'm going to tell these guys to leave. It's more interesting to recall the times when I enjoyed being with you, and I don't want any intruders."

The three men left after my uncle spoke to them.

"Let's go to where your dormitory is. It's easier to talk there because no one will interrupt us like yesterday."

We went into the dormitory, which was almost empty. There were only two people.

"How empty this place is! Only those two men and you live here."

"No, there are twenty-three of us in total. It seems like the others went to have breakfast. I feel safe here, you know... It feels as if we are all family. We were all in the Peruvian Embassy. Believe it or not, we have been fighting for your freedom, everyone else's, and our own."

"Explain that to me. What have you all been fighting for in terms of our freedom?"

"It seems you haven't heard."

"Heard about what?" I began to briefly recount how we left Cuba and everything I went through. The beatings I had to endure from the communist guards. He listened to me very attentively and I saw that he was amazed.

"Nephew, you're quite a hero! You bravely risked your life to get so many of us out!"

From that moment, he treated me differently. I was his favorite.

The next day, we saw each other again. Like the day before, he was waiting for me at the dormitory door.

"Good morning, uncle."

"Good morning, nephew," he replied with a smile. "How are you this morning?"

"Good, and you?"

"I feel better than ever!"

"Uncle, why are you so happy today?"

"If I tell you something that happened, you won't believe it!"

"What happened?"

"Yesterday, when I went to my dormitory, a soldier was waiting for me. He told me that one of my women, whom I had in Cuba, is claiming me. She used to visit me when I was in prison. But I didn't think she would dare to come to this country. And now she's here. Now she's sent for me. Don't worry, if I get out of here first, I'll help you get out as soon as possible. I'll do everything I can. I'm telling you this in case you don't see me anymore. Take care, because there are very bad people here and lots of prisoners."

We went inside the dormitory, and there were some guys playing cards. They were betting cigarettes. In that refuge, they gave cigarettes to adults, I don't know how many. My uncle, seeing them, decided to join the game and tried to teach me, but I wasn't interested.

"Uncle, I'm going for a walk," I told him. "You keep playing."

"Okay, but be careful. And remember what I told you."

"Alright, but don't play the mother with me."

My uncle shook his head with a smile and continued playing with the guys. I went to my bed to leave some cookies. I went outside, and before leaving I heard shouting, maybe it was the guards. I started walking quickly. Then my uncle noticed my nervousness.

"What's happening, nephew?" he asked me. "I think there's a scandal," I said, a bit surprised. "I can't believe that after going through so many problems to get to this country, now I don't have a little peace either. I'll go see what's happening."

"Wait for me, I'll go with you. Because now that I have someone to trust, I don't want anything to happen to you. Besides, I have to watch your back just like you have to watch mine. I wondered, 'why does this man, who is my uncle, care about me? If he never did before.' "

Outside there were many men and among them also many homosexuals. I had never been among so many prisoners and homosexuals. I felt a bit scared. I decided to walk slower so my uncle could catch up with me.

"Rolando! Rolando! Rolando, it's me, your uncle!" he shouted, approaching me.

I was so deep in thought that I didn't hear, and on his last shout, I reacted.

"Why are you shouting at me, uncle?"

"I shouted because you were out of this world. I was calling you and you didn't pay attention. But I'd like to know what you were thinking. Of course, if you can tell me."

"I didn't realize."

"I thought you'd lost your senses. I thought you were paralyzed. Nephew, I don't want to be too intrusive, but when you calm down, I'd like you to tell me, even if it hurts a lot. Maybe I could help you with something."

I didn't answer him anything. We went out to see what was happening. Outside there were many men running and shouting:

"Freedom! Freedom! We're tired of being imprisoned! Freedom! Freedom!"

We saw that the men were very rebellious, and some were already fighting. My uncle turned around and saw that one of his companions was running toward us, as if fleeing from someone.

"Ricardo! Ricardo!" my uncle shouted. "What's happening?"

"Come! Come with me!" the boy replied, stopping abruptly.

My uncle looked at me hesitantly. I understood his attitude.

"Go, go with him, because I'm going inside. I don't want more problems. I've had enough in the Peruvian Embassy."

My uncle went with that man and further ahead they stopped to talk. Fifteen minutes later, my uncle returned.

"What's happening with these people, uncle?" I asked him a bit puzzled. "Why now that they're free, do they decide to do this? I think they're going to ruin everything."

"What happens is that these fools have been imprisoned in Cuba all their lives," he told me without any importance. "They are used to living with homosexuals. They have believed they are their women, to the extent that now they are fighting over it."

"But, why are these people overturning the military's cars?" I asked him again, a bit confused. "They act as if they are still imprisoned. Don't they know that the important thing is that they are now free from Fidel Castro's dictatorship?"

"Look, nephew," he said, trying to excuse them. "These people are ruining everything they have gone through in our country. Look, the only thing you need to do is not get involved in these problems. You'll see that, if they continue like this, they will get what they deserve. Just watch and see. Come, come with me to see what's going on."

We started walking. The first thing I saw were three men beating a young man. It seems that the young man was taking the "girlfriend" of one of the attackers. On learning of the betrayal, he went to seek him out with two other guys and carried a machete.

My uncle, seeing what was happening, wanted to separate them, but they ignored him. One of the attackers took the machete and swung at the young man twice. He missed both attempts. On the third attempt, the desperate young man tried to take the machete from the attacker, but the attacker slashed his hand almost in half. When he saw what he had done, he fled quickly. We found a piece of sheet and tied it around his hand. Then we took him quickly to the infirmary. When we entered the place, we saw another man who had his throat slit.

I had seen violence, but never as much as that day. The military couldn't control the situation. In the Red Cross clinic, I saw several wounded bleeding out, all because they were with their enemies. And this was the place where they came to settle old scores. It seemed unbelievable to me that after being free, they still did these things. They didn't care about dying or leaving the shelter in good shape. For a moment, I thought the officers would come and take us all to jail, including me and maybe others who had nothing to do with what happened. While we were waiting for them to attend to the young man we brought, several wounded men entered. "Here comes another one! And what will they do to him? It's not possible! If we're already free, then, why are they shouting FREEDOM? I don't think they want to go to jail again. Crazy!"

"Well, I came just to accompany you because, in reality, I don't know this friend of yours. I hope they attend to him quickly so that he doesn't lose more blood. I'm going to my barrack because I don't want more problems. I'm tired of them. Besides, neither you nor I have anything to do with it. So let's leave or, if you want to stay, stay. I'm leaving."

"All right, nephew. I'm staying," he told me. "Go to your barrack. Try not to get into trouble. See you later."

I left that clinic on a very beautiful summer day. What I liked the most was seeing those beautiful mountains surrounding the camp.

"Why do I have to go through so many things like these to achieve what I want? It's true what my mom used to tell me... 'You have told me that to get what one desires costs a lot and the price must be paid.' I just hope I have already paid everything so as not to owe anything. I believe that this is how my opportunity to get out of here will come, although it's very beautiful. But I want to know more beyond this."

I returned to reality when people started running, trying to escape. The military was trying to calm things down and seven or eight men were overturning the military's vehicles. The car tires were facing upwards. Some soldiers were pulled down from the vehicles so they could overturn the jeep. Several prisoners took advantage of the occasion to go to the family zone. Others I did not know where they went. The military called for reinforcements and only then did they control the situation.

I waited a couple of weeks for my uncle, but I never saw him again in that shelter. Three weeks later, some soldiers came looking for me.

"Are you Rolando Castillo?" they asked me.

"Yes, I am," I answered.

"Do you have any relative here?"

"Yes," I answered, thinking they were referring to my uncle Gregorio. "Come with us," they said as they walked, and I went with them.

Upon arriving, I saw it was another uncle of mine on my mother's side. When I saw him, I recognized him immediately.

That uncle had been more present in our lives until a year before. I felt a great joy seeing him because I no longer felt alone in this country.

"What are you doing here, Uncle Rolando?" I said and I hugged him.

"Don't worry for now," he answered. "Later we will have time and we will talk calmly. But first we will see what these people will do with you and then we will talk. The military called me and asked me some questions."

"Do you know this man?" an officer asked me.

"Yes, yes I know him," I responded immediately. "Where do you know him from?"

"From Cuba!" I answered. "He is my uncle, my mom's brother."

"Alright, kid," they said.

"Sir, let us see your identification," the guard asked my uncle.

"Yes, sir. Allow me, I'll show you immediately," said my uncle while taking a black wallet from his pocket. "Here it is. Take it."

The guard checked his name and then returned it to him.

"If we can't find a sponsor for you," the officers told me, "then your uncle will take care of you. In this case, if your uncle agrees, there won't be any problem."

"Yes, I agree to take care of my nephew," said my uncle.

After leaving the office, my uncle and I talked for a long time.

"Ronaldito, how did you get to this country?" my uncle asked me curiously. "You know I came to check the lists to see if I knew anyone and I was surprised when I saw your name."

"I came on the boats that arrived a month and five days ago," I answered.

"But I hadn't seen you. Where have you been all this time?"

"Well. The first three days I was in Key West. And from there they brought me here. Hey! Come here. Since I arrived at this place, I always check the lists of those who arrive and those who leave, and I never saw your name."

"Maybe because I arrived before you."

"Yes! That's why. But tell me, how did you get a sponsor?"

"It was all thanks to a friend who already left here. Before leaving, he told me he would find me someone."

"Where is your sponsor from?"

"He is from Santo Domingo. By the way, he has a wife who is from Puerto Rico, her name is Gloria. I'm going to ask her to sponsor me. I think she will accept."

"Really? I hope so! Because I'm eager to leave this place. It's nice, but I want to explore beyond."

"I understand how you feel. Many times I've felt that same desperation."

"Uncle, where is your dormitory?"

"My barrack?"

"Yes, your barrack."

"It's in zone four."

"But that's for families and single women!"

"Ah, I haven't told you. Look, a month ago there was an uproar in this shelter and they turned the military jeeps over. Perhaps you saw it. I took advantage of that situation to move to the area where I am now. There I met a woman and now she's my girlfriend. We are living together as a couple."

"When you leave, will you leave her?"

"I don't want to, but I have to. She already knows and accepts it. Let's change the subject. Tell me, how is your mother?"

"I thought you were never going to ask about her."

"With the excitement of seeing you and talking about the sponsors, I forgot to ask you about your mom earlier."

"When I left, she was fine. I don't know how she is now. I didn't have time to say goodbye to her. Days before, she was very sad because I was going to leave."

"Don't worry too much about that. I know your mom and I know she's very strong."

I felt a little sad and decided to change the subject. It was getting late, and I retired to my dormitory.

The sky was blue and cloudless. The mountains surrounding the shelter looked beautiful. The sun shone and the air was fresh. In the distance, some very pretty houses could be seen. I watched them for a while, trying to see if I could spot anyone.

"What will the people be like here? Will they be friendly, kind? I think so because at least the soldiers here treat us well. I wish my mother was here with me to see this beautiful place. I hope she's alright and not worried. I had to come so I could have everything I never had since I was little. I won't tell my Uncle Rolando how I came. I won't. Just remembering it makes me want to cry."

"Look, boy, where we drop you off, you're going to run fast because if you don't, you'll miss the plane!"

"How cruel! They knew I would never catch it because it was already twelve. What bullies!"

"I'm leaving and I won't sign anything."

"My dad, still being so stubborn."

"You don't know what you're saying! But alright, wish him all that. You don't know if he'll get out of this alive," the police told my sister.

"I got out of that alright! I made it. That means a lot to me. It's one more opportunity to do something in this life. Just remembering, it makes me angry with those police... What will happen with the little boy who the dog tore a piece of flesh from? His leg so small and that animal bit it so fiercely."

"And my uncle Gregorio, where will he be? The important thing is that I already found another uncle. At least he isn't a convict. Hmm! Speaking of that... I remember that my Uncle Rolando was put in jail several times, only for days or weeks. It was because he's anti-communist. Yes, I remember. How the communists called us! Scum, traitors. Go away, we don't want you. But we didn't want them either. That's why we are here. Away from communism! Free!"

After seeing my uncle I felt more confident. Every day I would visit him. We were together all the time.

"Ronaldito, do you remember when you were little you used to play tricks on me?" asked my uncle.

"I remember some things," I replied. "Not everything."

"When I would visit, your mom sometimes had you punished because you were terrible. But you didn't care about the punishment because you'd escape without your pants. Then she'd say to me, 'Rolando, go catch that boy who's escaped again'. I'd run after you and when I'd catch you, you'd kick me really hard, in the lower parts! You'd leave me lying on the floor."

"I don't remember that," I told him.

"No! Of course you don't remember, because it doesn't suit you!"

"Really, I don't remember that."

"Do you know what else you used to do to me?"

"I don't know."

"Before I caught you, you'd throw stones at me! And one day you hit me so hard that you opened my head and I had to get three stitches. And the best part, without anesthesia!"

During the days we were together, I laughed a lot at what my uncle told me. Maybe he did it so I wouldn't miss my siblings and especially my mom so much.

"I think I was four or five years old, and one day my mom tied me to the leg of the bed so I wouldn't go out into the street. I was so bad that I said to my sister... Was it Mari or Mercedes, I think it was Mercedes? To give me a knife, but she couldn't quite reach the drawer with the utensils. And I was desperate to get out. Then I remembered that in a corner of the garden, there was a piece of glass. 'Mercedes, bring me the glass that's over there in that corner!' I told her, pointing with my finger to the spot. She gave it to me and with that, I cut the cord with which my mom tied me and I left. That day my uncle wasn't there because otherwise, he would have come after me to catch me. And the day I slipped away to go with some men to help them with their business. They gave me a bag of money to go to the bank to change it for bills, and being distracted, the bus almost ran me over. I wonder: What if, because of my disobedience, the bus had run me over? I wouldn't think because I would have caused my mom great pain.

"Will my mom have money? It's been more than a month since I left and I don't know how my family is doing. For now, my uncle is with me, but when he leaves... I'm going to feel alone again. Where is my uncle Gregorio? I haven't heard anything about him. I had a good time with his company, but it's better with Rolando because he's not as addicted as Gregorio. If I don't say! Jail has taught him a lot.

"I don't know how much time passed while I was remembering a series of events from my childhood.

"Hey Ronaldito, you never told me how you came to be here," my uncle said to me. "The other day I asked you, but with the conversation, you didn't say anything."

"Well, I came on a shrimp boat," I replied.

"Yes, but what made you come here?"

"Oh, I don't know... it just occurred to me."

"I don't think it was because of politics, was it?" he said, trying to get me to say something.

"No. You know I wasn't into that."

"Yes, I know, that's why I'm asking," he insisted curiously. "Or did you get into politics?"

"No, I told you. I don't like politics."

"Did you come to this country because you wanted what?"

"Look uncle, I came here because I wanted to see another place."

"Mmh, it's just that I see you very sad... I thought they had kicked you out."

"Why do you think that?"

"Because on your own, you wouldn't be here. Look son, I remember you only working to help your mom. And would you do anything else before leaving her alone?"

"Yes, that's true. That's why I'm here. I want to have money and send it to my mom so she doesn't lack anything. That's good what you want. Tell me one thing, exactly, how did you come from Cuba?"

"Well, like you, like everyone. By boat! Now that all those people left. And how did you come?"

"They took me out for being anti-communist. You know how Castro is. If you're not a communist, you're a criminal and a traitor to the country. Besides, the committee people were always watching me, to see if I wasn't doing something against that man and his government. Imagine me doing something bad! Not even thinking about it. I'd be dead by now."

"Sure you would. If I didn't know."

"Why do you know?"

"Because of everything I've seen done to other people."

"Ah! I thought you were involved in something like that!"

"No! Uncle, that's not for me."

10
MY FREEDOM

"Look Ronaldito," my uncle told me, "I think they are coming to get me out of here tomorrow. But I promise I'll come back for you."

"Did they tell you you're leaving?" I asked.

"Yes, they sent for me to verify some data."

"That's good. Because you're almost out. But I don't know when I'll get a sponsor."

"Don't worry," he commented, "that's what you have your uncle for."

Being in the shelter I already felt bored and annoyed. I needed to get out of that place. My hope was that my uncle Rolando would really find me a sponsor. I know he wasn't like my uncle Gregorio. The latter had promised to come back for me and didn't do it. Perhaps what helped me was that in that shelter there were various activities to keep us distracted. They showed us different movies every week, gave us English classes, and the priests would come and talk to us, explaining about the Bible and God.

However, because of the situation I was in, I didn't pay much attention.

The next day my uncle's sponsor and his wife arrived. They took my uncle to the office, and from there he went out to the street. I saw when he left and I couldn't help but feel a lump in my throat.

That night I couldn't sleep, thinking about my family. When will I manage to get out of here? What will become of me when I am outside? I think the worst thing a person can feel is loneliness. And worse in a country where another language is spoken. And where you don't know anyone. And you want to talk and you can't do it. Sometimes I tried to forget that I was alone again in that place. However, nostalgia and depression made me cry. Then I hid from people so they wouldn't see me cry. I knew I wasn't doing well. That to survive it is necessary to be very strong. Many times due to my sadness I thought it was a mistake to be in this country, that I shouldn't have left my family. That I should have never inquired about the Embassy, that I felt alone and depressed... that I had to be strong. The solution I found to my mood was that, cry without anyone seeing me. I couldn't trust anyone, but I also didn't have anyone to do it with. I never did it with my uncles. Because I was ashamed and afraid that they would make fun of me. That's why I preferred to keep my feelings to myself.

Despite knowing a guy who used to sit almost in front of where I took a seat. We started talking and became good friends, but I didn't trust him.

He was from another dormitory. And whenever we talked it was about the homosexuals who lived with the inmates. And that several times they dressed in a very shameless and daring way. A week after my uncle left, they informed us that those who wanted to go to Australia should fill out an application.

Luis and I, that was the boy's name, went immediately to fill it out. They promised to give us the response in three weeks.

"Look, I think it's better to go to Australia," Luis told me.

"Yes, I think so too."

"There must be people there who are also in our situation. And it might even be nicer," Luis commented.

"Never mind the nice part, what I want is to get out of this place to anywhere. Because I'm already tired here. I want to see other places."

"I feel the same way."

"Well, and besides that, we have the opportunity to study to be electricians. That's a good opportunity. Don't you think?"

"The day they had the meeting I didn't understand very well. I thought they were going to give us electrician jobs."

"What are you thinking? Without knowing anything!"

"Of course. I thought better of it later. And it seemed impossible."

"Look, what we need is already there. Now we just need them to tell us when we're going there."

"I hope it's soon. Like you say, I don't want to stay in this place either. It's nice, but I don't know what's wrong with us."

"What's wrong with us, Luis, is that we aren't free. We live here and I thank all these people. But I don't want to have walls or bars preventing me from going where I want."

"What bothers me besides my confinement is that bunch of faggots. We see them every day going back and forth, well hugged with the inmates. And besides, the way they dress, they're so daring! Look, I'm not a macho, but I'm old-fashioned and I see it as wrong," Luis told me a bit annoyed.

"Me too. They raised me the old way, and what those faggots do doesn't please me at all. The worst thing is that when they pass near us they flirt like women. And they've even said things to me. Although I'm not interested in what they say, as long as they don't come straight to me, it's all good."

"Well, I don't like it either. I don't pay attention to them, and I better go somewhere else. Because you see that they always blame one, like if one was the one provoking them!"

"That's true. You see how they are. They are always in trouble."

"By the way, Rolando, what if your godmother comes to get you before? Would you go to Australia or rather stay here?"

"It's what happens first. If they come for me first, I'll go. But if they send us to Australia, then I'll go there."

Two weeks after I accepted to go to Australia, the military came for me at the dormitory.

"Look, kid, they want to talk to you in the office," the officers told me. "Come with us!"

"Is it about Australia?"

"I don't think so," an officer told me, "but now they'll tell you."

We arrived at the office, and my heart fluttered with emotion upon seeing my uncle along with his godfather and his wife.

"How are you, little Ronald?" my uncle greeted me.

"Good, uncle," I replied, full of joy.

"Look, we came to visit you and also to introduce you to Mrs. Gloria, because she is going to be your godmother."

"What? Are you sure about what you're saying?" I responded to my uncle, very surprised. "Did she agree to be my godmother?"

"Yes, son. I spoke with my godfather, and he told her. And look, she accepted! Oh, because she is my godfather's wife."

"Yes, you told me that, right?"

"Yes, I told you. Come, follow me, I'll introduce you to her."

"Look, Gloria, this is my nephew, the one I told you about."

"Nice to meet you... What's your name?"

"How are you, ma'am? My name is Rolando."

"Very well. Do you know that I will be your godmother?"

"Yes, ma'am, thank you!"

"Well, now all that's left is for them to tell me when we can come for you."

"I think it will be soon, son," my uncle said happily. "In the meantime, try to behave well like you have been and follow the orders as best as you can," she told me.

"You seem like a good boy, and I'm sure you are," the husband of the woman who would be my godmother told me.

"We're leaving now, and remember, we will come for you," my uncle told me.

"Rolando? And when will your godmother come for you?" Luis asked me, a bit sadly.

"When the officers speak to her and tell her everything is ready."

"What are they preparing?"

"Some papers that my godmother has to sign."

"They came two days ago, right?"

"Yes, I hope it's soon."

"And what if we hear from Australia first?"

"Well, I'll go there. Because if my godmother's thing takes long, I'll go to the other place. I wouldn't want to stay here longer."

Luis and I were talking, and some officers arrived at the dormitory where we were.

"Well, boy, are you ready to go to your new home?" the officers asked. When I heard that, I turned and saw they were addressing me. I was surprised, not knowing what to answer. My companion got happy. We hugged and wished each other good luck.

"Rolando! I'm glad you're leaving. I wish you lots of luck!"

"Same to you, and I hope they send you to Australia soon." Suddenly, tears came to his eyes seeing that his only friend in that shelter was leaving.

"If I ever have the opportunity to succeed as I've always wanted, I would spend whatever it takes to find you so you could be my business partner, even if you had no money."

"I thank you very much for being my friend. And I will never forget those words. I would do the same if God allowed me."

"Well, boy, do you want to go or stay?" the officers asked, already tired of waiting. "Even though it was just a few minutes, we're waiting too long, and you're not the only one we have to look for. So let's go now, please."

"Look," I told Luis, "I have to go. Best of luck to you!"

I couldn't help it, and I cried too. That farewell was very sad because that boy was in the same situation as I was. I got into the jeep they had and they took me to the office in zone five, it was a place of complete families. There were many immigration people.

"Come, boy," an immigration officer said, leading me to a separate desk.

"Yes, sir," I replied, following him.

"Look, boy, this is a work permit," he said while handing me a badge. "With this, you can work wherever you want to. Now go to that office, they'll give you some things there."

"Thank you, sir," I shook his hand and said goodbye to him.

I went to the office he indicated, and when I entered, they gave me some clothes.

"Look, boy, this is so you have something to start looking for a job. Later, you can buy whatever you need."

"Thank you for everything," I told them.

At that moment my uncle appeared, along with my godmother and her husband.

"Hello, nephew!" my uncle said, giving me a hug.

"How are you, uncle!"

"What's up, little Ronald!" my godmother greeted me.

"How are you!"

"Congratulations, boy!" her husband approached. "Now you will come with us!"

The lady had two children, a girl and a boy. By the way, the boy was deaf-mute.

The immigration people finished all the procedures. Afterwards, my godmother and I were given several papers to sign.

"That's all. Boy, good luck," the officers told me. "You can go now! Take this opportunity!"

As we left, we headed towards their car, and I saw that a tall, handsome boy got out. He opened the door for us. The car was very nice, it was an '80 Chevrolet.

"I'm going to ride in that car! It's so beautiful! I can't believe it! I've never been in a car like that!"

"Who is that boy, Mrs. Gloria?" I asked her when I saw the little boy.

"That's my son, the one I told you about last time," she replied, as my uncle was speaking too. "I have another daughter, but now she's in Puerto Rico."

"How am I going to communicate with the boy when we're alone, if he neither speaks nor listens! I must watch how they do it! Maybe that way I'll learn!"

I got into the car and it was very comfortable inside. I looked and looked at it, it was the first time I saw such a new car.

"When I work, I'm going to buy myself a car as beautiful as this!"

My godmother was driving the car and I was looking through the window. It wasn't that beautiful, but since I was already free, I saw everything as gorgeous! I watched everything and felt happy. I was enjoying it when I saw people. They looked strange to me. And everything was so different from my country. We arrived at the apartment where they lived. I felt safe. It was then I knew I was starting a new life, without knowing that after fighting so much for the long-awaited freedom, my fate would be very painful and difficult. I then began to struggle tirelessly in a world so different from mine and, worst of all, facing it alone.

11

LIKE A CRIMINAL

The apartment was luxurious and big. My "godparents" gave us a room for my uncle and me. The area they lived in was very quiet. The nearest neighbors welcomed us very kindly, despite not speaking the same language. There I met an American girl, whom I liked, and she liked me. Although that relationship didn't work out because she liked to go out with her friends and play a lot, something I found in very bad taste since I was used to my girlfriend going out only with me, and the customs here are different. I forgot about her. Another thing that unsettled me was that my uncle liked our "godmother."

In the same house, my uncle flirted with her and she reciprocated. I didn't like it because I was very grateful to her and my "godfather" for contributing to our freedom.

"Ronaldito!" my uncle told me one day. "Look, nephew, your godmother is a little in love with me."

"Look... uncle," I replied, "Don't say that! I'm sure she doesn't even notice you. She has her husband and she loves and respects him!"

I responded like that to see if my uncle would drop the issue and let them live in peace. For me, it was a hypocritical and cowardly act to take someone's partner, especially when that person has given you support and trust to help you be better in all aspects. My uncle was so happy he looked like a young man. According to him, he would have a new car and money if she decided to be with him.

"Ronaldito," my uncle whispered one night, "You know? I just thought of something!"

"I think I'm going to be with her," he answered, "To have everything I want. Besides, she earns good money."

"Uncle, what you're doing isn't right," I told him, "Because that man has done you a tremendous favor by getting you out of the shelter. And it's not fair to him! He trusts you! And with no interest."

My uncle laughed as if everything was funny. I was getting desperate, and he got mad at me.

"Are you with me or not?" he asked.

"Yes, I'm with you. But..." I replied, "You're getting into a big problem, and I don't want to be in the middle of all this."

As he behaved, I always knew he would never offer me his help or give me good advice, much less would he ask if I was okay or not. My godfather got drunk and argued a lot with my godmother, maybe because he was jealous since she was very sweet and pretty. Meanwhile, I decided to look for a job and save to move out to avoid all those problems between them. Luckily, a friend of my uncle got me a job in a chicken shop. I dedicated myself enthusiastically to that job. Later, my uncle and I began to contribute some money for rent and household expenses, even though the government gave my godparents some money to cover our food needs while we were at their place. When I had some free time, I accompanied my godmother to the supermarket, and she taught me English words, as well as explained some customs of this country.

One day, when I was bored, my uncle invited me to walk to the town of Pottstown.

"Nephew, let's go to town," he said, "So you can meet other people. There are many Hispanics there!"

"Let's go," I replied, "It'll help to distract me and know a bit more about this town."

In the village, I met a man named Ángel Sierra, and he introduced me to his family. He had four daughters, five sons, and his wife. I realized that everyone in the village knew them, and I learned that it was because several years ago, he was the chief of police in that place.

From then on, I became good friends with the family and visited them very often. I found out that one of his daughters was being abused both physically and mentally by her husband.

It was a Wednesday, and we were chatting in the living room when suddenly I heard someone crying. Suddenly, his daughter came in.

"Dad! Pepe hit me and threw me out of the house!" the daughter said, crying.

"But just look at how that miserable man left you!" Don Ángel replied. "Daughter, I've told you not to go back with him. Look, go to your mother so she can put something on your face."

The daughter went to her mother's room, who didn't even know what was happening.

"Ronaldito! Come here," he said, beckoning me with his hand, "Come here, I need to ask you something. I don't know if you will agree... but..."

"Tell me, Don Ángel," I said, approaching him.

"Look, listen to me carefully," he said in a low voice, "Every time that man hits my daughter, I feel like taking him down. I don't want my daughter to keep suffering with that individual. You know, I love my daughters very much, and I wouldn't want that man to give her a bad blow one day and lose her forever."

"And what do you want me to do?" I asked, interrupting him.

"Teach him to respect a woman," he replied, "I'll make sure to reward you. Look," he said, showing me a package of money, "You'll take this money, it's five thousand dollars."

"And if your daughter finds out about the beating I'm going to give him?"

"Don't worry," he replied, "I'll handle it."

"Tell me, Don Ángel," I said, a little curious. "Is it worth hitting that man? Because your daughter will continue with him. And if your daughter finds out that you sent someone to hit her husband, what position will you be in?"

"Don't worry," he replied. "She won't find out. I just want him to know that punches hurt. So just send him to the hospital, don't kill him!"

"When do you want me to do it?" I asked.

"Right now!" he said impatiently. "Take one of my cars. Make sure he doesn't see who hits him. Look at this photograph so you'll recognize him. Oh! Here's the key to the apartment where my daughter lives. That idiot is probably drunk there."

"Don Ángel? And if they ask about me," I said, "what will you tell them?"

"I'll take care of that," he replied. "I'm sure they won't know where you went."

I went directly to the apartment where the daughter lived. I didn't take any identification in case I got caught. I left the car a few blocks away. I took a bat that Don Ángel had already prepared, and before entering, I put on a mask. I opened the door. I peeked in and saw that he was deeply asleep with a woman.

I approached slowly and moved him. He woke up and looked, half-opening an eye. I didn't give him time for anything!

"This!" I said, giving him a blow on the arm. "Is so you won't abuse women!"

At that moment, he looked at me and wanted to defend himself, but it was too late.

"To show you that punches hurt," I said, hitting him on the other arm. "To be exact, on the elbow."

"Ouch!... who are you? Ouch!" he was saying. "Don't hit me anymore! Ouch!"

"Take this! This is what you deserve!" I replied, hitting him in the ribs. "Women should be treated well, not with punches!"

The woman who was with him got up and tried to defend him, but I hit her behind the ear, and she fainted. I gave the man a couple more blows to the ankles and then turned my back and left.

I arrived at Don Ángel's house and saw that everyone was calm. The man just looked at me, and I signaled to him that everything had gone well. He approached and discreetly gave me the money. Suddenly, the phone rang.

"Hello?" asked Don Ángel. "Who do you want to speak to?... Daughter?"

"Daughter Rosita," he shouted, "it's for you on the phone!"

"Who is it, dad?" she asked, intrigued.

"I don't know, they just say it's urgent," the man replied.

"Hello?" the girl answered. "What? What do you say? Where?"

She started to cry. The father, with a certain tone of surprise, asked what was wrong with her.

"It's the police!" the girl replied. "They say Pepe is hospitalized! That he was beaten up!"

"What?" exclaimed the man, pretending not to know anything.

"Yes," she replied. "Maybe he went out drunk and someone beat him."

"Are you going to see him?" the father asked her. "After what he did to you."

"You know I'm going to go," the girl replied, very upset.

"But daughter," the father said, "do you see? Your famous husband, instead of avoiding problems, he creates them for you.

Even when you're not with him! And he always finds a way to convince you and drive you away from us."

“Dad,” she said, “you're going to start with the same thing again!” I was listening to the conversation and decided to interrupt.

“Sir,” I said to him, “if you want, I can take her, no problem.”

At that moment, Don Ángel realized that I was doing it so that his daughter wouldn't find out that we were involved with her husband's beating.

“That's fine, young man,” he answered quickly. “That sounds good, take the keys to my car and take her.”

When we got to the hospital, I realized the young man had casts on his stomach, hands, and feet. I felt bad for what I had done, but I needed the money.

Two months later, I decided to move out of my godmother's house, and the money Don Ángel had given me, I slowly saved in the bank. My godmother didn't want me to leave, nor did my godfather, but it was necessary to do so.

In the end, my uncle stayed with my godmother, and my godfather was kicked out of her house. She didn't realize that my uncle only wanted her money, aside from wanting to show his friends that he could conquer any woman. And my godmother was only with him not because he was good-looking but because her husband argued a lot with her, and they weren't entirely happy.

Anyway, I felt bad because that betrayal shouldn't have been done to my godfather since he helped us to get out of that shelter.

It was two in the afternoon when I saw my godmother saying goodbye to a coworker with a kiss on the cheek. I took advantage of that fact to tell my uncle that she said goodbye with a kiss on the mouth.

“Ronaldito!” my uncle said indignantly. “Are you sure she kissed him on the mouth?”

“Yes, uncle,” I replied very confidently. “I saw them!”

“If you're so sure...” he told me, “I'm going to bring her so you can say it to her face!”

The next day, he took her to where I lived. When I had her in front of me, I stood by what I said, creating a separation between them. I felt good after my lie since that's what I wanted. All because I knew that my uncle only wanted the money and nothing else.

“Look, nephew,” my uncle told me, “the money has just slipped through my fingers. But it doesn't matter because there must be more out there, it's just a matter of looking!”

I lived in a small room. I felt lonely and then needed to go out to find my friends. I went into clubs and one day I met a light-skinned woman, she was African American. She was pretty. We started dating and ended up living together. During that time, I realized she was very aggressive. One day, she arrived upset and, in front of her grandmother, insulted me.

“Rolando,” said the grandmother very angrily, “if you don't hit that woman now, you won't come back to this house! Because I love you very much and I know you are a good boy. And she takes advantage of you because she knows you love her!”

I was so angry that when the grandmother told me that, I obeyed and gave her a hard hit. And then we broke up. From then on, the brunette dedicated herself to finding me and insulting me.

During that time, I had a friend who was Puerto Rican. Her name was Mary. Thanks to her advice, I didn't suffer much when I broke up with the brunette, who, by the way, was named Loran.

On December twenty-fourth, Mary, some friends, and I went to celebrate in a bar. Around midnight, several people arrived and greeted my friends. I heard someone say something, but I didn't pay much attention.

“But look who's here!” said this person, almost shouting and already drunk. “Is it true? Or am I seeing things?”

I felt someone place their hand on my shoulder and turned around. Then I saw it was my uncle Gregorio.

“Does he know you?” Mary asked, a little surprised.

“Yes, he's my uncle!” I replied happily.

“Nephew! Come! Come closer!” he said while placing his hand on my shoulder and taking me to another table. “When we leave here, let's go to my apartment, because I have a little surprise for you.”

“What surprise?” I asked, a little doubtful, since I hadn't seen him since the shelter.

“Shhh! Shhh!” he replied with that sound. “Don't let them hear you!” After midnight, we went to his apartment.

“Look, son, I'm going to bring you what I promised,” he said as he headed to his room.

He returned after five minutes.

"Uncle, what do you have in your hand?" I asked, seeing he had something in his right hand.

"Look, son, see this little bag," he said, laughing. "Look at it well!"

It was a small transparent plastic bag and contained a green herb.

"Uncle, what is that?" I asked.

"It's marijuana!" he said with a smile. "You and I are going to smoke it until we're wasted!"

"No, not me. Look, uncle, I've never tried it, and I'm not interested in doing so."

"Don't tell me that," he answered mockingly. "If I know your girlfriend... that Loran, smoked marijuana! Didn't you know?... And didn't you accompany her to smoke?"

"Yes, I knew," I replied, "but I told him not to do it in front of me, and I never smoked it!"

"I don't believe that you don't smoke," he said somewhat incredulously.

"No!" I replied. "I didn't even know it."

"Well, here you will learn!" he responded as he made a cigarette. "You're going to like it! It's something different!"

"No, uncle! I don't want to do it!" I told him.

"But what do you mean you don't want to?" he replied. "Look... we men are brave, we are strong, not cowards! So... prove it!" After talking for quite a while about whether I should smoke it or not, I ended up accepting. Besides, I drank beer. That day I got completely lost.

I woke up at eight the next morning. I immediately looked for my money and verified that it was complete. That distrust was because of the people who were with us that day and whom I didn't know, even though they were friends of my uncle. Once I verified that my money was intact, I washed my face and tidied my hair a bit. I left there and went to my apartment to get a bit more sleep. I was awakened by loud knocks on the door.

"Who is it?" I asked half-asleep.

"It's me," replied a woman's voice that was unfamiliar to me.

"Wait a moment!" I shouted as I put on my clothes. "I'll open the door in a minute!"

When I opened, I found a very cheerful and pretty girl.

"Who are you looking for, miss?" I asked her.

"I'm looking for a Cuban who lived here a few months ago," she said as she peeked inside.

"Well, no other Cuban lives here," I replied. "And I just moved to this place."

"Yes, I see. It's just that, you know... he was my boyfriend," she said to me, "only I had to go to New York and we stopped seeing each other..."

While she spoke, I listened very attentively. I looked at her face, a bit sad when she told me about her boyfriend. I kept thinking, "Look, Ronaldito, most women here are not thinking about anything serious, so don't get involved with any of them."

"Hey?" she said to me. "Are you listening to me?"

"Ah! Yes! Yes," I replied immediately. "But come in and take a seat!"

She entered and sat down. I assumed she wouldn't because we didn't know each other yet.

"You know, let me wash my face, because I was asleep," I told her as I headed to the bathroom.

When I came out, the woman was staring at me intently with a flirtatious air.

"Is something wrong with me?" I asked her.

"No, why?" she replied.

"Because you're looking at me without taking your eyes off," I said to her.

"It's just that from the first moment I got a good look at you," she responded, "you've really made a good impression on me."

"How strange!" I said to her. "You don't even know me yet! Nor do you know my name!"

She very coquettishly replied to everything I asked her.

"I know who you are," she told me. "And I lied to get here."

"What do you mean you know who I am?" I said intrigued. "Tell me what game is this?" I asked.

"You want to know if I know you, right?" she asked, laughing.

"Yes!" I replied somewhat desperately because she was laughing and I didn't know what her plan was.

"Well, then... Your name is Rolando and your uncle's name is Gregorio, isn't it?" she asked me.

"Yes," I said, "that's true, how do you know? Who are you? What's your name?"

"Ah! I forgot to introduce myself," she said laughing. "My name is Katy."

"Your name is Katy? Okay, Katy," I said a little distrustfully. "You're Puerto Rican, aren't you?"

"Yes, I'm Boricua," she replied to me. "Is there something wrong with that?"

"No!" I replied. "I asked because of your accent, which is different. But tell me, how do you know me?"

"Through your uncle, I told him I liked you," she said to me. "And he gave me your address. And I planned how to introduce myself to you."

We talked for a while and it was already night, she made no attempt to leave.

"Katy, don't you plan to go to your house?" I asked her, surprised.

"No, what I want is to stay with you," she replied decisively.

I didn't know what to say, it took me by surprise.

"Katy... but... what about your family?" I said a bit disconcerted.

"My family?" she replied with some disinterest. "What do you want to know about them?"

"What will they say?" I said to her.

"Nothing, they don't have to say anything. Besides, I live with my grandmother," she replied, laughing. "And she will have to accept it, whether she likes it or not!"

I was left thoughtful about her response: "Here women do what they want, and everything stays as if nothing happened. But it's the liberation women talk so much about! Hmm... If this were to happen in Cuba, poor my sisters! My mom would have broken their heads!"

Two days passed and then she decided to go to her house.

"Ronnie, accompany me to my house," she said to me.

"Okay, but I'm not going in," I told her. "Because I don't know what your grandmother might say."

"Nothing, she won't," she said unconcernedly.

Once at her house, I heard her talking with her grandmother.

"Katy! What do you mean you're leaving?" asked the grandmother. "With whom?"

"Don't worry," replied Katy. "Rolando! Come!" she yelled at me, leaning out so I could see her.

"What's going on?" I asked her.

"Nothing, look, grandmother," she said, "he is my boyfriend, and soon we are going to get married."

I only greeted her, and Katy didn't give her time to ask anything, just said goodbye and told her she'd call her later.

"Katy," I said in a reproachful tone, "why did you tell her we were going to get married? You know it's not true!"

"Now you see why I never get married?" she said crying. "Because men, like you, only wanted me to pass the time."

I didn't know what to say to her. I felt like a scoundrel. We stayed silent until we reached the house.

"Well, after all, you didn't propose that she should stay, much less marriage. No! No! I'm wrong! Poor thing, go and cry. All because of what you said to her!"

We had already been together for two months, I worked at a chicken shop and didn't feel so lonely anymore. One day I ran into a daughter of Don Ángel and chatted with her for a while. She told me she liked a friend of mine and I decided to introduce them. Soon after, and to my surprise, they got married and bought a house. They rented me a room and I accepted. Katy and I moved in with them.

The house that Rosy and Manolo bought was nice, and the room they rented me was large with two big windows.

One day I found out that Manolo, Rosy, and Katy smoked marijuana. And what I did was go to sleep. One day the girl that lived with me convinced me to smoke and the four of us did it.

"Katy... I'm sorry for having smoked," I said. "I think I won't do it again."

"You say it like it's a bad thing," she replied. "In this country, everyone does it!"

"I don't think so," I responded.

"Of course they do!" she replied. "It seems you haven't lived much yet, huh?"

"Anyway, I won't do it again," I responded.

At the chicken shop, they paid me little. Katy didn't work because she said they paid too little. I never told her she should as I considered it ungentlemanly to say so. Seeing that I earned little money, Manolo and Rosy offered to help me get in where they worked. Two weeks later, I started at the factory with them. I didn't have very good luck, since the boss didn't like me very much and sent me to work in a place where I had my hands in water eleven hours a day, six days a week.

One Friday, Katy told me we should go to town for a walk and when we arrived I greeted a friend I found while Katy stayed in the car. Suddenly, I heard a woman's screams and turned around. I saw Katy running out of the car chasing a woman. It was Loran, the brunette who had been my girlfriend.

"Katy! Wait!" I yelled as I ran after her.

"No! Let me give this woman what she deserves!" she told me. "Because she yelled a series of insults at me that I don't like!" I caught up with her and stopped her. She was very upset and I decided to return home.

When we got home, I saw Rosy's father.

"Don Ángel! How nice to see you here!" I said. "Sorry I can't stay with you for a moment, but I have something to resolve."

"Don't worry, boy," he replied. "I see your girlfriend is very angry. Go and talk to her."

I entered the room and she was yelling really loudly. I tried to calm her down, but it was all in vain. That day she left and I decided to go to the bar to have a few drinks.

12
EASY MONEY

After three days, when I wasn't there, the Puerto Rican girl returned. She left a note stuck on the door. It said:

"I want to see you urgently, because I have something for you, with which you will never have to work again."

That note left me thoughtful and as soon as Rosy and Manolo arrived, I asked them if they knew anything about it.

"Rosy," I asked, "did Katy tell you anything about this note?"

"Let me see," Rosy approached. "Mhhh... pay attention to what I'm going to tell you because I care for you like you're my brother. Katy isn't good for you because the day she left here, she went straight to New York to get drugs to sell and now she wants to involve you."

I was speechless in astonishment. The first thing I thought was: "Why does this have to happen to me? I don't want to get into trouble because of drugs and even less with the law in this country. Could it be that since I'm alone and don't really know the way of life here and besides I don't know English, do these women want to take me for a fool? It seems like almost all of them are criminals!"

"I think I won't see her anymore!" I told Rosy.

"That's the best thing you can do," she replied, "because besides not working, she used your money to buy marijuana to smoke." I tried not to see her again. She frequented the house but I was never there.

"Hi, Rolando!" Rosy greeted me. "By the way, today Katy was here and my dad offered her a job and she accepted."

"To work where?" I asked curiously.

"Taking care of Laurita," he told me. "Do you remember her?... She's the old lady my dad protects."

"Ah! Yes, I remember her," I replied.

"Do you know something else?" he asked me.

"No. What?" I said, trying to find out.

"That Katy was flirting with our boss," he said.

"Really?" I asked, amazed. "Now I understand why the boss treated me so badly since I started working! Hey... do you think she slept with him?"

"We don't know," he said, "but the boss told me she was very clever, and she's only after money. But he didn't do anything because it would ruin his marriage."

I never saw Katy again. One weekend, Rosy, Manolo, and I were having some beers. I noticed my friends were trying to tell me something, but they didn't know how.

"What's wrong with you guys?" I asked. "You're hiding something from me, right?"

"I'm going to tell you something that might upset you," Manolo told me while Rosy went to her room. "Don't take it to heart."

"What are you going to tell me?" I responded.

"Katy was kicked out of Rosy's parents' house," he said.

"That doesn't bother me," I said. "Why was she kicked out?"

"Because she started flirting with his dad, you know, for money. And Rosy's mom caught them naked in the room they had given her to live while she took care of the old lady. You know she was paid very well, but she lost everything for being stupid."

I was happy because at least I knew I would never see her again. That day I took a shower and went to the bar where we friends used to meet. I arrived there and ran into a cousin of Rosy's whom I knew.

"Hey, 'brother,'" he greeted me.

"How are you, Polito?" I said, using his nickname, since his name was Paul. "Why are you so happy?"

"Because my sister just came back from Puerto Rico," he told me. "She lived there for a while and now she's back."

"And who is your sister?" I asked. "Because I think you brought her to this place, right?"

"She's the one sitting in the chair over there," he told me while pointing to where she was. "But don't you dare do anything with her, because she's not for you, okay?"

"Just introducing me to her," I replied, "doesn't mean I'm going to be with her."

"Okay, let's go," he replied. "I'll introduce you, but no funny business, okay?"

"Okay, Polito," I responded.

She was with another sister they called Rina.

"Look, Lorena," Polito said to his sister, "he's a friend."

"Nice to meet you," she said, smiling. "My name is Lorena."

"Nice to meet you. My name is Rolando," I replied. "Do you want to dance with me?"

"Yes, of course," she said as she got up.

"Rosy, I want to ask you something," I said.

"What do you want?" she replied. "What do you want to ask me?"

"About your cousin Lorena," I said. "I already met her. Why hadn't you told me you had a cousin?"

"Well, because she was in Puerto Rico, as far as I knew. She's no longer there. They introduced her to me last night," I replied.

"And when did she arrive?" she asked, surprised.

"I don't know," I said. "But she's pretty."

"If you like her, I'll help you with her," she said.

"Yes, I like her," I replied with excitement. "And if you help me, it's even better."

At work, they changed my position. At least I no longer had my hands in water all day. They assigned me to cut the tendon of the pigs and put them on a line that would take them to another department where they would remove their hair. I arrived at the factory in the morning and started working as I always did. I took a pig and turned it to cut its tendon. The floor was wet. Suddenly, I slipped. I felt like I cut something, but I didn't know what it was. I got up and looked at my left hand because I felt something trickling down. I saw that my pinky finger was missing. I didn't feel any pain, maybe because my blood was hot. I looked at my hand again and then noticed that the finger was actually hanging from a tiny piece of flesh. I immediately went to the offices and told the secretary what had happened to me.

"Did you cut off a finger?" she asked incredulously. "Let me see, move your other hand to see your finger."

"Look," I said as I showed her what had happened to me.

"Oh, how terrible... God..." she said nothing more because she fainted.

The boss sent me to the hospital immediately with Manolo. When we arrived at the emergency room, they made me wait more than six hours because the doctor who had to treat me wasn't there. I almost fainted from the pain and because I had lost a lot of blood. Finally, the doctor arrived and apologized. He took me to a room with a table soaked in a dark liquid and put on some gloves. He started cleaning my hand with a gauze.

Subsequently, she took a dark thread and a needle and sewed my finger without anesthesia. In total, she gave me sixteen stitches. I had unbearable pain and she only prescribed some pills that did nothing for me, as I couldn't sleep. At six in the morning the next day, I went back to the hospital because my hand was too swollen and black and bluish.

"Miss, I need to be seen," I told the nurse. "Because yesterday afternoon they sewed this finger and my hand is in bad shape and it hurts a lot. Look... See how it is."

"Allow me, sir..." she said and headed towards a room. I stayed there standing and she quickly returned to where I was.

"Look, we'll let you see a doctor and he will attend to you immediately," she told me.

They took me to an office and the doctor was already waiting for me.

"Let's see, young man," he said. "Let me see how your hand is."

"Doctor, it hurts a lot, see," I told him and showed it to him.

"Young man, we're going to have to operate on you," he told me. "Because your hand is in very bad shape."

"But... yesterday a doctor sewed my finger," I said.

"Yes, I know," he replied. "You arrived in time to save your hand."

"Are you going to operate on me now?" I asked.

"No, until tomorrow," he said. "Because we have to run several tests on you first. At noon the doctor came to see me. The next day early I was operated on."

"Young man," he told me. "The reason for that infection was because of some pig bristles. You had them inside! Didn't they clean your hand properly yesterday?"

"Well, the doctor cleaned me with a gauze and a dark liquid and then sewed me," I replied.

"Well, he didn't clean it properly," he responded.

My finger was left bent and I couldn't straighten it. I went through that for six years. I couldn't work, and I decided to sue the factory. Meanwhile, with my savings, I bought a car for four hundred seventy-five dollars. Since I wasn't working, I went to various places and one day I met Polito.

"How's it going, Rolando?" he said to me.

"Good, Polito," I replied. "What do you do for a living?"

"My business," I responded.

"What business?" I asked, curious.

"Well, I bring merchandise from New York," he replied. "And I sell it here."

"By the way, would you like to travel with me over there?" he asked with interest.

"Well, I'm not sure," I replied.

"Come on, it's worth it. It's nice, and you get to know the place," he was saying. "And I'll pay you to take me. How does that sound?"

"Let me think about it and then I'll tell you," I replied somewhat hesitant.

"Alright," he said. "Tell me later what you decided."

Fifteen days later I saw him and I said I would accompany him to New York. We agreed on my salary and I became his driver. That's how I met another man called "Lizard." I never knew his real name and he also came with us, paying me for taking him. We went very often.

"Polito, tell me why you go to New York so often," I asked him.

"Look, Rolando, I'm going to tell you the truth," he said approaching me. "I go to get drugs. I get them cheaper there and when I sell them here, I make a little over double. And without over-exerting, do you understand? Nice and slow."

I watched all his movements and started to learn how to negotiate to get more money from the investment.

On one occasion, we met a man who had several people working for him. They distributed the drugs and later handed over the money.

"Look, young man, I would like you to work for me," the man said.

"But I still don't know much about the business," I replied.

"It's not necessary. All I want is for you to make some trips," he told me.

"Let me think about it and then I'll tell you," I responded unsure.

"Alright, if you accept," he said. "You can see me in Pottstown."

He handed me a small folded piece of paper. "Look, it's worth it. You'll earn more than what your friends pay you." This man awakened my ambition and I was about to say yes to him.

"Okay. Maybe we'll talk another day," I said and got up from the chair. "See you soon."

"I'll be waiting for you," he replied. "Don't think too much about it."

Two days later we returned to New York. Polito didn't want to return with us and stayed at a half-sister's house. "Lizard" and I got ready to return. We stopped at a traffic light, and suddenly six youngsters stood in front of the car; one of them pulled out a gun.

"Give us the merchandise," they shouted at us. "Quick! Give us the merchandise!"

"What do we do?" I said in a low tone to my companion.

"Step on the gas in this car," he responded. "And don't stop until we hit the highway."

Since I liked all those things, I stepped on the gas and only heard shots.

"Lizard! Are you okay?" I asked.

"Yes, and you?" he asked me.

"I'm okay too," I replied.

That's how we escaped from those guys. I still think the same ones who sold "Lizard" the drugs sent them.

The next day I checked my car and saw that it had three bullet holes. That day was Saturday and "Lagartija" was having a birthday. Some friends and I agreed to throw a party for him. That way, they would also take the opportunity to sell their drugs. The party took place on Sunday, and since that day all the nightclubs and bars closed early, people kept having fun in the basement of the house we had rented. From that day on, every weekend we threw parties and also the number of people increased. We earned four thousand dollars per night, as we sold fried chicken, pork, beers, and liquor, plus we were well organized. Some watched the door while others took care of the drinks and food.

Seeing that everything was going well, I decided to invest money in drugs and sold them at the parties. That way, I managed to triple the money I invested. We were all happy with the business until one day a new Cuban arrived in town and we recklessly invited him to participate in the business. Soon after, he began to impose his conditions and wanted to boss us around. However, in the group, there was a guy who didn't like what that man was doing, and they started arguing.

"Look, ace," Miguel said to him with the typical Cuban expression. "Neither I nor anyone here likes you giving us orders in such a short time. Besides, we only invited you to help you earn some extra money. So start settling your accounts."

"You're nobody either," the man replied very angrily. "To tell me what I have to do."

Suddenly, the man pulled out a revolver, and Miguel pulled out another one. Then they went out into the street and started shooting at each other. It looked like the Wild West in the year 1983. Luckily, neither of them got hurt. As a result of that problem, we decided to end that business, although after a while they started having parties again.

I almost didn't sleep at Rosy and Manolo's house because I was busy with the business, but one day I decided to go to their house.

"Rolando!" Rosy shouted at me, surprised. "What happened to you that you almost never come to sleep at the house anymore? We thought you had forgotten about us!"

"No, it's not that," I said. "You know how our parties are, they never end!"

"Will you stay today?" she asked curiously.

"Maybe yes because I want to leave around twelve," I replied. "Rosy, tell me something."

"What is it?"

"What's Polito's sister like?" I asked anxiously.

"Why do you ask?" she said.

"Because I like her and also because Polito calls me brother-in-law," I explained. "He suddenly started calling me that."

"Maybe he actually wants you to be his brother-in-law," she replied with a satisfied air, as she knew I liked her cousin. "I can't tell you what she's like because I haven't seen her in a long time. But if you want, one day we can go see her and you can talk to her, what do you think?"

"That sounds good, we'll arrange it later," I said. I went to my room and fell asleep. The next day I had to collect money for the drugs the guys who worked for me were selling. Román was my direct assistant, and he was in charge of giving me the money the guys made from selling the merchandise I gave them.

Very early I went to Román's house and he wasn't there.

"Good morning, ma'am," I greeted his wife. "Is Román at home?"

"No, he's not. Maybe he'll be here tonight," she said.

"Thank you. I'll come back to see him later," I said goodbye and went to where I knew I could find him.

That day I couldn't find him, as no one knew where he was. So I thought about going to the man who offered me a job one of the times I took Polito on his trips.

"How are you, sir?" I said. "I'm here to ask if your offer is still available."

"Sure, young man!" he said. "Have you made up your mind?"

"Yes, I think so," I replied. "I'm finishing some business, and then I'll be free."

"Alright, I have a trip in twenty days," he said. "And for that trip, I'll pay you fifty thousand dollars, and if you do well, we'll pay you up to a hundred thousand dollars on the next trips. Do you agree?"

"Yes, I agree. When should I call you?"

"Call me in ten days, and then I'll give you instructions." I said goodbye to him. Leaving his house, I went to a friend's house where there was a gathering. We stayed up all night there, and then I remembered I had to collect my money from Román.

13
THE DEATH

It was around seven in the morning when I arrived at the house where I lived. From afar, I saw there were many police officers. I parked three or four houses before mine. Rosy, Manolito's wife, came out from among the people and approached me.

"Rolando! Rolando!" she shouted at me. "Guess what, they killed Román."

"What did you say?" I asked, astonished.

"They killed Roman," she repeated to me. "And it seems it was the 'Flaco'! They found Roman's body in the trunk of his car, and who knows since what time. They shot him four times in the chest," Rosy told me in tears.

I couldn't believe what they had done to Roman. I reacted and approached the car. Rosy was right, it was Flaco's car.

Shortly after, I went to the supposed murderer's house and found his wife.

"Good morning, ma'am," I greeted her as if nothing. "I came to see your husband. Is he home?"

"No, I haven't seen him all night," she quickly said with some nervousness.

"Ah, okay," I said, as I looked toward the street to see if his three cars were parked on the sidewalk. I realized there was only one. There were always two there because Flaco drove one of them. "Well, I'm leaving. When he arrives, tell him I came to see him."

"I will tell him," she replied hastily and immediately closed the door.

I realized she was protecting him. However, I didn't want to investigate further. So I left there as quickly as possible because sooner or later I knew the police would show up.

When I got to where I had parked my car, I saw four police cars arriving. They started to surround the house. They lived in the apartment on the ground floor. Meanwhile, I got into my car and watched what was happening from there. Five minutes later they came out taking Flaco's wife detained.

"There's nothing here. Hmm, I'm going to search the closet. Damn it! There's nothing here either. I hope in the drawer..."

Suddenly a shoebox fell. I opened it and saw that there was the money. It was like ten thousand dollars in cash.

"I hope they didn't see me when I came in. I'm sure they didn't. I checked that no one was there. No, no one saw me! The best part is that the police forgot to close the windows. That damn 'Flaco', he only did it to take the money. And the money wasn't Roman's, it was mine! But even so, I'm lucky."

Actually, when they took Flaco's wife away, I saw that the balcony was open and that's when I got in.

"I'm going to hide the money in the underwear. Just in case they see me! I'm not carrying anything. I'm going to leave through... No, not through the balcony again. No! Someone could see me. Better go out through the back door. I hope it's unlocked."

I left the house and headed towards my car. I drove away from there. "I don't know why Flaco had to do that to Roman. There were many ways to solve the problem they had. I imagine death is the last alternative, and it's not even an option. It's just not right. That fool just left three kids without a father. And his wife, poor woman, how did she love him?" Many thoughts were coming to my mind as I drove home. "Damn Flaco. Too bad he's Cuban like me. But to that guy, I would put two pressure clips on his private parts and then shock him to see if he likes it."

The day they buried Roman, it was a cloudy day, it really looked sad. I think the pain of his relatives was so great that it even reflected in the weather that day. It was a bit windy, and the tops of the trees swayed from side to side. I drove down the main driveway of the cemetery. The grass was green, it looked like a big carpet. I don't know why in cemeteries the grass is always green, perhaps because our bodies, after death, give it life, since when we are alive we always make sure to destroy it in some way, either by stepping on it, pulling it out and sometimes drying it when we don't feel like watering it. I moved forward a little more and parked the car.

In the distance, on a small hill, I saw the group of people dressed in black. I approached slowly. Upon arriving, I saw that his wife was sitting next to the coffin, among the people. She was completely unrecognizable. For a moment I thought she was an old woman. She looked emaciated and very thin. She was wearing dark glasses and still, her aged face was noticeable, it was because of the pain of having lost her husband.

I felt deeply moved. I approached slowly, making my way through the people.

When I reached where she was, I shuddered to see her children crying inconsolably. I put my hand on her shoulder, and she turned around.

I didn't know how to tell her that I brought the ten thousand dollars I rescued from the house of her husband's killer. At that moment it crossed my mind that if I told her that, she wouldn't take them because it was from the executioner who ended her husband. So I decided to say something else, the first thing that came to my mind.

"Ma'am, I'm very sorry for what happened to Roman," I said in a soft tone. "Look, this money... is for you to have something to start with. I mean... without your husband... maybe you need to work... I'm sorry. Maybe... you'll need it later."

"I don't need money," she shouted at me. "I want my husband alive. And I can no longer have him. It's all because of you, who were the ones who killed him."

When she told me those words, I also felt guilty. I joined her in her crying, because it hurt me a lot what she said, in addition to the suffering that woman felt for her husband.

In that small village, they mourned greatly on the day of the funeral, as that man was known by many people and very loved for being a good man and highly respected.

Three weeks had already passed since Roman's death, and I was still bothered by what they had done to him.

Since the day of his funeral, I promised not to involve anyone else in selling drugs for me. I decided with more determination to work with the man who had previously offered me a well-paid job for each trip to New York.

"Rolando, what's wrong with you, boy?" the Don said to me over the phone. "I have a job for you, this coming Friday."

"Alright," I replied confidently. "Tell me when and where."

"That's why I'm calling you, boy," he said. "It's tomorrow. I need you to come today. I'll give you the address." That day I went to "Lizard's" house to ask him to accompany me, as I didn't know New York well.

"Hey, how are you, 'aceré'?" I said using that Cuban expression that means friend to us.

"And what brings you here?" he replied. "It's very early to come."

"Nothing, 'aceré'," I said casually. "I just came to tell you to come with me to New York early tomorrow."

"Yes, of course," he answered immediately. "Because I need to go too!"

"Ah, well! If that's the case, let's go!" I said with pleasure.

"Hey, are we coming back tomorrow?" he asked anxiously. "Because I need to be here tomorrow."

"Don't worry about that," I said. "We're coming back tomorrow."

"What time exactly do you want to leave?" he asked.

"At five in the morning," I told him, because I didn't know the exact time I needed to be in New York. "Because you know I like to arrive early at places I don't know. Meanwhile, I'll inspect the place we are going to."

"You're right. Although I know New York very well," he said confidently. "Let's get ready! Besides, I also need to go. But tell me, are you going for the same reason as me? And on your own?"

"Stop asking questions," I replied a bit annoyed. "We're going, right? It's convenient for you, isn't it?"

"Yes, yes, it's true," he said, agreeing with my response. "After all, it's convenient for me."

"Well, 'aceré', I'm leaving because I have something to do," I said goodbye heading towards the door. "Be prepared!"

"Yes, don't worry about that," he said, closing the door almost at the same time.

I headed to the Don's house for him to tell me what I needed to do and give me the address. That day, the people who guarded him checked me from head to toe before letting me in.

"Come in, boy," he said smiling, putting his hand on my shoulder. "I knew you wouldn't back out."

I entered a study with a large bookshelf covering the entire right wall. On the left side, there was a mahogany wood desk, with a black leather chair, and in front of the desk, two mahogany chairs with black leather seats and backs. Parallel to the door was a large window with an excellent view of the back garden. I remember the few times I went to that house they served to know some parts of it.

It had an indoor pool, in the garage there were five cars, and in the room where the living area was, there was a huge well-lit spittoon, thanks to a window offering a view of a distant mountain. The armchairs were made of black leather, there were two lamps in the corners whose bases were ivory with black silk covers. When they were lit, they were lovely and were on black mahogany tables that matched the coffee table, on which there was a magnificent Chinese porcelain vase with gold details. "If the Don lives this way, without working properly, why can't I achieve it? Of course, I can also live like this."

"No, I told him I was interested, and besides, I'm a man of my word," I replied.

"I know, that's why I proposed the business to you. Sit down, you're at home," he said, while walking toward a door located to the left of the desk that, when opened, connected with a well-lit hallway. "Jaime, bring the package!" he shouted to a boy who immediately entered the room we were in, carrying a small package in his hand. "Give it to Rolando."

The boy handed me the package and left. I looked at the Don, waiting for him to tell me what I should do next.

"Here is the address and they're expecting you there at ten-thirty in the morning," he extended his hand to give you a folded paper. "You will give them that package, just as I give it to you, and they will give you another one."

"That's fine. I'll do it that way," I replied, saying goodbye to him. "See you tomorrow night, okay?"

"Yes. I think you come back around seven or eight at night. I'm telling you in case you want to go somewhere else. Just be careful," he replied.

"As you say," I bid farewell again. "See you the day after tomorrow!"

I called "Lizard" and told him we could leave later.

"'Lizard,' hey 'brother,'" I said. "We're not leaving at five in the morning. I'll pick you up at seven. Are you ready?"

"Why, 'brother'?" he asked.

"Because I have to be here until ten thirty," I replied. "Ah, then that's fine," he said. "See you tomorrow!"

The road to New York was calm and the trip was pleasant. We arrived in New York and "Lizard" started guiding me to the place where the package had to be dropped off.

"Look, turn right at that corner," he told me.

"And from here, where to?" I asked after turning.

"Turn left on the next street," he said. "And it's roughly the fourth or fifth house."

"Yes, it was complicated," I said. "It would have been very difficult for me to get here. What time is it?" I asked him.

"It's ten fifteen, we barely made it in time," he told me. "Yes, that's true," I replied.

I got out of the car and looked at the house. It was two-storied, with three steps leading to the main entrance. On the right side, a thick glass window appeared to belong to the basement. I climbed the steps and rang the doorbell. To the left, there were two windows, one on the first floor and another on the second. There was a passageway next to the house, which I imagined led to the backyard. While they were opening, I was observing the house.

The door opened, and a man peeked out.

"Look, I'm here on behalf of..." I said, but the man didn't let me finish.

"Yes, come in. We know who you are," he said as we walked down a hallway. Initially, on the left was the staircase, followed by the living room on the right, then the dining room, the kitchen, two consecutive closed doors, and at the end, we reached a study. Inside was an older man.

"Come in, boy. We've been expecting you. Hand him what you brought," he told the man who opened the door for me. "You have something for us, right?"

"Yes, this is for you," I handed over the package and took mine.

"Tell 'Don' that we're in touch," he told me.

"I'll let him know," I replied. "See you later!"

I left the house. Afterwards, we went to have breakfast. At half-past eleven, we went for "Lizard's" merchandise.

"Let's leave early to get there soon. You see that the trip is long. And there's nothing else to do here," I told "Lizard".

"Yes, let's go, because you know I need to be there today," he said seriously. "They're waiting for me. You know, I can't let them down."

"Rolando, here's your money," Don told me. "Thank you. It's just that now I need you to give me a couple of weeks to clean this money," I replied.

"That's fine, but don't back out on us," that man told me. "Because you know how to handle our work."

"No, trust me," I told them. "Thanks and I await your call." I put the money in a small bag to avoid drawing attention. I immediately went to rent an apartment a friend recommended. He used to rent that apartment, but since he moved to another town, he had to leave it.

I went home to drop off the money and rest, as I hadn't done so in a long time. Upon arriving, I found Rosy and Manolo.

"Rolando! Where have you been?" Rosy said to me. "We were worried about you, because you know what just happened with Roman."

"Don't worry, you know I just go from party to party," I answered laughing.

"Rolando, what do you have there in that little bag?" Rosy asked me. "Is it a gift for me?"

"No, it's not for you," I replied. "But if you want something, just ask."

"The only thing I want is for you to lend us your car," she said. "Because it's been a long time since Manolo and I went dancing, and now we want to go to the disco to dance."

"Sure thing. What time will you bring it back to me?" I asked. "Because I'll need it tomorrow. Look, before anything else, I want to tell you something..."

"Something you don't know if we'll like?" Rosy repeated.

"Yes, I want to move out of here," I said. "And I plan to do it first thing tomorrow."

"And where are you going? Do you have a place to move into?" Rosy asked, somewhat hesitantly.

"To an apartment I just rented a little while ago," I said.

"As far as I'm concerned, that's fine," she replied. "Because I talked about you to my cousin. You remember her, right?"

"Yes, of course, I remember her," I replied excitedly. "What did she say about me?"

"She told me that she really likes you," he replied. "But also that she has a son, and if you accept him, you can talk to her. If you come to an agreement, she could visit your house. You know, she's at my other cousin's house and doesn't feel well. She has problems because every time she goes out, she leaves the child with my other cousin and he's mistreated. Well, sometimes that's how family is. Hey! And I think Manolo doesn't agree with you leaving, right Manolo?" Rosy asked her husband, but he acted like he didn't hear. He turned around and left.

"Rosy, I am the owner of my own life," I said to her. "And I don't have to ask your husband for an opinion to do what I need to do. Now I have to go faster because I don't want to cause trouble with him."

"All right," she said. "Don't say anything and wait for us to return. In the meantime, collect your things to avoid problems."

They left, and agreed to return at midnight. I looked at the clock and it was already one in the morning and they still hadn't returned. I wanted to go to the bar, but without the car, I couldn't do anything. I got tired of waiting and fell asleep. When I woke up, it was six-thirty in the morning. I got up from the bed and took a shower.

I left my room and went to look for Manolo, but they still hadn't returned. When they arrived, it was seven-thirty. Rosy entered first.

"Weren't you supposed to arrive at midnight?" I asked her seriously.

"We ran a little late, you know. You meet old friends and time flies," Rosy told me.

"And Manolo? Where is he?" I asked.

"He's outside, he'll be in shortly," she said. "Meanwhile, I'm going to my room."

Manolo came in and I greeted him. I noticed he was a bit drunk.

"What's up, 'aceré'?" I said to him. "I've been waiting for you. Look, I need my keys."

"No, I'm not going to give them to you," 'aserré' replied.

"Come on! I'm not in the mood for jokes," I said laughing. "I want to go out."

"No, 'aserré', it's not a joke," he replied annoyed.

"Why don't you want to give them to me? That's my car!" I said very angrily.

"If you want them, come get them," he said showing me the keys with his hand extended towards me.

"All right," I replied approaching him and trying to take them away.

I approached and we struggled. Suddenly, he punched me in the face and I, angry, threw him. At that moment, there was a glass ashtray weighing over three pounds on the coffee table. I grabbed it and was about to smash it over his head, but something inside me said, "No, don't do it. You'll get into trouble for nothing." So I decided not to do it. Rosy noticed what happened and came down immediately.

"Manolo, please! Give him the keys," she said as she approached. "Give him his keys, they're his, for his car!"

Rosy very angrily took them from him and gave them to me. "No matter what you do, you won't be able to stop him from leaving,

Rolando has already made a decision and neither you nor anyone else will change that."

While they argued, I went to my room, gathered my things, loaded them into my car, and left for my new apartment. I arrived, took a shower, and fell asleep.

14
SOME ENCOUNTERS

I was standing at the door of the house observing the neighborhood. There was a restaurant in front. To the right corner was a laundry and a supermarket. I was hungry and decided to buy something to eat. As I was crossing, I saw a woman who looked like my uncle Gregorio's girlfriend. I didn't pay attention and went into the restaurant to eat. I left the place and decided to stroll around the area. When I returned and was about to enter my house, I heard a voice calling me.

"Rolando! Rolando!" shouted the voice.

I turned and saw my uncle's girlfriend. She was waving her hand at me. "Wait, Rolando," she said approaching me. "You're Gregorio's nephew, right?"

"Yes, I am," I replied. "What's up?"

"I need to talk to you, but... alone, somewhere else," she said. "Not on the street."

"Okay, if you want, let's go to my apartment," I replied. "There we can talk quietly."

"All right, let's go," she replied.

We headed to my house.

"I rented this place yesterday, that's why I don't have anything yet," I said when I saw she was surprised to see there was no furniture. "Ah, sorry, I couldn't help my surprise," she replied. "You know, when one enters a house, one always expects it to be furnished and that's what I expected here. But... this is better than living on the street."

"And my uncle, where is he?" I asked.

"Don't you know what happened to him?" she asked me. "No, what happened?" I said intrigued.

"They put him in jail," she replied. "He got arrested for selling drugs. He's been in jail for almost nine months. But he's getting out next month. Well, bad luck," I replied. "I know what the problem is with you. You want me to help you until my uncle gets out, right?"

"Yes," she replied excitedly. "I'll help you clean and cook, or I'll cook and clean while you work."

"I'm not working," I replied. "Don't you see how my hand is?"

"Yes, I noticed, but I didn't dare to ask you."

"Well, I'm going to help you until my uncle gets out of jail. And I'm doing it because... you're pregnant, right?"

"Yes," she responded.

"Look, what I don't like is chaos in my house," I said. "I also don't want you to bring anyone here."

"Yes, that's fine," she replied. "I agree with you. Now I'm going to get my clothes. And thank you very much!"

That same day, I met a friend we all called "the Chinese." He invited me to his house, and I accepted.

"Rolando, I want you to help me," he said to me. "I'm broke."

"How do you want me to help you?" I asked.

"Let me sell drugs, and I won't let you down," he said desperately. "I can't help you there. Look, I already got out of that," I told him. "A while ago, you know, since the Román thing."

We were talking about that when there was a knock at the door.

"Who could it be?" he said. "I think it's that bitch."

"Who?" I asked.

"A woman I was with," he replied angrily. "She doesn't leave me alone, and I don't want anything with her anymore."

"Well, tell her that," I replied. "I already told her, but she doesn't understand," he said. "Hold on, I'm going to see what she wants," he said and got up to open the door. When he opened it, I saw the girl had a glass in her hand and threw something in his face. My friend screamed and covered his face. At that moment, I got up and saw the girl running away. Meanwhile, the Chinese collapsed and was almost unconscious from the pain. I picked him up and took him to the emergency hospital. Then I found out she had thrown sulfuric acid in his face. The terrible thing was that it got into his eyes. When I saw him again, I realized he lost an eye, and his face and neck were marked by the acid.

"You know, Rolando, despite everything, I'm happy," he said to me. "Because that woman got arrested. And now I'm happy with another woman."

"That's good. Hey, Chinese," I said. "Good to see you. Look, I need you to find some people to work with me fixing houses. Because I have a truck I just bought precisely for that. If you help me, I'll give you ten percent of the merit."

That's how he did it, he found me four Mexicans who knew construction very well. He started paying them two hundred dollars. We were hired to paint and fix an apartment. It all started very well, although things got complicated later.

I always tried to make sure they had work. When I made a trip to New York, I'd buy them a box of beers and a pizza, or whatever they wanted, as a token of my appreciation for their good work. Plus, I guaranteed them employment.

On one occasion, I decided to give them a day off. I invited them to a club that was very famous. When we arrived, the first thing I saw was Rosy.

"Hi, Rosy," I said happily. "How are you?"

"How are you, Rolando?" she replied.

"Is Manolo coming with you?" I asked.

"No, I came alone," she said. "Manolo let me come alone. By the way! I have a surprise for you! I think you'll like it."

"What surprise?" I asked. "Come on, tell me! Don't leave me intrigued. Don't laugh and tell me."

She laughed, and suddenly I felt someone behind me. I turned to see who it was. It was her cousin. Immediately I felt a chill run through me, and my hair stood on end. I didn't know what to do. I reconsidered and calmed down.

"Hi! How are you, Lorena?" I said. "I'm glad to see you!"

"I'm fine, and you?" she replied.

"Good, good," I responded with some timidity. "What would you like to drink?"

"I want rum and Coke," replied Rosy.

"And I want a piña colada," said the cousin.

"Well, I'm going to the bathroom and I'll bring the drinks," I said a bit nervously.

When I returned, I saw them laughing and talking about me.

"What are you laughing about?" I asked them. "Are you making fun of me? Am I so funny that you're laughing?"

"No, no," Rosy replied. "It's just that my cousin likes you, and you like her too, right? Only she's shy."

I invited her to dance. That night I talked with her and had a pleasant time. I found out from Rosy that Lorena was with a married man, but he didn't promise her anything.

"Yes, Rolando, that's how it is," Rosy told me. "My cousin wants a man like you, who works and helps her raise her child. And who gives her a home to live in, because she lives with my other cousin and doesn't feel very well there."

"I'm going to talk to your cousin about that," I said. "I think I can help her. But I'm going to take that risk, because you know what happened to me with the other Puerto Rican woman, remember?"

"Yes, I remember," she said. "But with my cousin, that won't happen to you. Look, she is different. She's not like the other one. I never said it, but I didn't like that ex-wife of yours, because I know you're good. Look, if it weren't for Manolo, I would be your wife, because I know you. But it's too late for that. I wish you much happiness with my cousin and enjoy being with her, because I know she will say yes to you."

We finished dancing and then I remembered that I hadn't gone to that place alone. My workers were with me!

"Lorena, Rosy, may I have a moment?" I said to them. "I'm going to see the guys I came with."

I arrived at the table where my friends and workers were.

"Rolando! Did you just arrive and already have a partner?" one of them said to me.

"They are long-time friends," I replied.

"We're not stupid," said another. "But don't worry, we know how to respect."

"Well, guys, here you go to have some fun," I told them, giving them fifty dollars each. "Take tomorrow off, but I want you early on Monday. Here's your pay."

At that time, perhaps I wasn't perfect, but I always tried to be good to my companions. Every time I did, I felt good about myself and alleviated a bit of my loneliness, which was causing me a lot of suffering.

"I see you don't trust me much," I said to Lorena. "I hope you realize that I am a different person. I don't like to play with other people's feelings."

Rosy was watching us. Then she got up and went to dance. She took a long time to return; maybe she did it so we could talk comfortably.

"Lorena, do you want to dance?" I asked her.

"Yes," she replied.

"Is that your name?" I asked.

"Yes, that's my name," she replied.

"Do you have a boyfriend?" I asked curiously.

"No, I don't have... well, I'm seeing a guy, but he's married... but I'm going to keep seeing him. I'll leave him when I find someone who cares about me and my son."

"Do you have a son?" I asked. "Where is he? Because you're here, and I suppose you left him in good hands."

"Well, the fact that I'm here doesn't mean my son is just anywhere," she replied a bit annoyed. "I do care about him!"

"And who is your son with?" I asked.

"I left him in the care of my sister," she told me. "And I will pay her because she takes care of him for me."

"Alright, don't be upset," I replied. "I asked because I thought you had left your son with someone else, and it's not good to leave children with people you don't know for so long. But let's talk about something else, maybe about us. What do you think?"

"Well... alright," she replied.

I gathered my courage and started to woo her. She drove me crazy. She made me nervous, and I didn't know what to do or what to say. I felt good because I wouldn't be so lonely anymore, and the suffering I carried inside for not seeing my family would at least not be as intense. However, I never imagined that this woman would be the one to destroy my life.

That night we became a couple and dated for three weeks.

It was eight-thirty in the morning when I went to see her. I brought some flowers for her.

"Honey, today it's three weeks," I told her. "How about we go out for dinner and dancing tonight?"

"But... I don't have the right clothes," she replied. "And I don't have money to buy them. You know, I don't work."

"Don't worry about that," I told her. "Because we're going now to buy you clothes. Don't worry about money."

She agreed, and we went to the stores. She bought several outfits, and they all fit her very well.

We went into a restaurant for breakfast, and I ran into one of the friends with whom we did the business in the basement of "Lizard's" house.

"Rolando! Hey, Rolando!" my friend called while approaching where I was.

"How are you, 'acere'?" I responded with the classic Cuban expression. "And what have you been up to?"

"Nothing, 'acere'," he said. "Look, you don't know one thing! We reopened the basement! So if you want to go, you know where we are. Anytime you want."

"Alright, 'acere'," I said. "Maybe I'll go one of these days. I gotta go because I have things to do."

"Alright. Take care!" he replied. "I see you're accompanied. Is that your girlfriend?"

"Yes, that's why I'm leaving," I replied.

That night, I took her to dinner at a very romantic restaurant.

It had a very romantic blue light, and the walls were white. The tables were round, with white tablecloths, and in the center, there was a bouquet of white and red flowers on a blue basket, next to a candelabra with two red candles.

After dinner, we went dancing. At two in the morning, they closed the club, and I decided we should go to the basement to continue having fun.

"Rolando! What are you doing, 'acere'?" a guy said to me. "What's up, 'Gavilán'?" I replied, using his nickname.

"Is that Puerto Rican girl with you?" he asked me.

"Elia is my girlfriend," I replied. "Why are you asking me that, 'Gavilán'?"

"Mmm, just wondering," he answered with a mischievous smile that I didn't like.

I greeted several friends and introduced them to my girlfriend. The music they played was soft, and 'Gavilán' immediately came over to ask Lorena to dance.

"Lorena, do you want to dance with me?" 'Gavilán' asked my girlfriend.

She looked at me, as if asking whether she could dance with him.

"Yes, dance," I told her.

Soon she came back and the music wasn't over yet.

"What happened? Why didn't you keep dancing?" I asked her.

"No, that man was getting too close, so I left him on the dance floor for being cheeky. Besides, he told me I shouldn't be with you, that he was better than you. And honestly, I got mad because I didn't like the way he talked about you."

"Don't worry," I told her. "We shouldn't pay attention to people who try to get in our way. I think we're going to have to fight against everyone for our future."

We left the basement at four in the morning and went to my apartment. I decided to move to the basement of that house. My workers fixed up that place so nicely that Lorena liked it very much. Meanwhile, my uncle's wife lived on the first floor, and I paid her rent while my uncle was in jail.

That day went by so quickly that she didn't go for her son at that hour of the morning because the child was asleep, and we didn't want to wake him. Anyway, we slept so much that it was four in the afternoon, and she was already nervous. I also remembered that my uncle was getting out of jail that day.

"Look at the time!" Lorena told me. "I have to go get my son and for sure my sister is really mad! I promised to come back as soon as the club closed!"

"Don't worry, I'll go with you," I told her. "If your sister sees me, she won't be that upset."

"But... maybe she'll tell me to leave her house," she replied. "Because it's not the first time she's told me that! And I don't know where I would go. You know, I have nowhere to go. What do you want?" I asked her.

"I want my own apartment," she said. "And a man who is for me and cares about my son. Who makes me happy. Because I will serve him as a woman, and that's why... I chose you because I know you're not like the others."

At that time, I was looking for someone. I felt very lonely, and when she told me all that, she convinced me. I assumed she was the woman of my life and happily offered her my home.

"I know my sister must be very angry," she told me. "Because I left my son with her for so long. But I don't care. I won't lose you. And if anything happens, I'll call you. Wait for my call! Cheer up."

I arrived at the house and after greeting my uncle, I went to my apartment. Suddenly, the phone rang and it was Lorena.

"Rolando! Help me!" she said with a choked voice. "My son fell and needs stitches!"

She immediately hung up the phone and I went to her house. When I arrived, the ambulance was attending to him. He got four stitches on his forehead because his cousin had pushed him and the child fell down the stairs, hitting his forehead. At that moment, Lorena and her sister started arguing and they were so mad they hit each other. I had to separate them.

"Look, Lorena, pack all your things and let's go to my place!" I told her.

"But it's too soon to live together."

"Look, if you don't want to rely on anyone, come with me right now," I told her. "If you want to rebuild your life."

That's how we started. We got to my apartment and I heard shouting. I went upstairs to see what was happening, and my uncle was hitting his wife.

"Uncle, what's going on here?" I asked.

"Don't you meddle in what doesn't concern you," he replied, very angry.

"Look," I said, "this isn't your house to do whatever you please."

"Fine. Then I'll take her out on the street," he stupidly replied. "And do you want to go back to jail for abusing your wife?" I told him.

He remained silent and left.

"Ma'am, why were you fighting?" I asked the woman.

"Because he found out I was seeing another man while he was in prison," she replied.

I've never understood why I always witnessed these kinds of problems. First with my uncle Rolando and now with my uncle Gregorio. I guess that's why I always tried to stay away from them.

However, they always found me, I don't know how. And I couldn't deny them my help. They were my family. Although as such, they never responded to me. Never, as I recall, did they ask me about my mood. They never knew whether I had enough to eat or pay the rent. Thank God, I never lacked a plate of food or a roof over my head. During that time when I was making so much money, I tried to bring my family, but nobody wanted to come. I begged them too much, and they didn't want to. My mother told me she would never leave her children. That she'd rather suffer for one than for seven. Maybe she has always been right.

I went back to my apartment. The phone rang.

"Yes? Hello" I answered.

"Rolando, is that you?" they replied.

"Who's speaking?" I asked.

"It's me," the voice answered. "It's Jaime, the 'Don's' assistant."

"Ah! What's up, 'dude'?" I said. "How are you?"

"Good, I'm calling to tell you that we need to talk to you," he said.

"Do you have something for me?" I asked.

"Yes, come right away," he said.

I immediately went to the 'Don's' house. They were waiting for me and immediately gave me all the details. The next day, which was Monday, I had to be in New York. Fortunately, it was in the same place I went the first time.

I told Lorena that I had to go to New York for a business deal with a friend.

"What kind of business?" she asked.

"We want to make contracts there for painting and fixing houses because they say they pay very well," I replied.

That afternoon I took a bath, ate, and put on some clothes. I said goodbye to Lorena and went to see my workers.

"Juan, I'm counting on you to take the truck out early tomorrow and go with the guys to finish the job we left pending," I told him. "I have some things to do, but I'll be back in the afternoon."

"Alright, Rolando! Count on me."

From there, I headed to New York. I arrived after midnight. A man was waiting for me.

"How are you, young man?" he said.

"How are you?" I replied. "I'm here on behalf of the 'Don'."

"Yes, I know, I know you already," he said.

"Where is the package that I need to take?" I asked.

"Come over here," he said, walking towards an alley almost in front of the house. "Do you see that plastic trash bin? Inside there's a crumpled paper bag, and inside that bag is the package."

When he told me that, I immediately parked the car next to the bin, got out, pretended I was checking the car's tire, and quickly loaded the package into the car. I got in and saw the man was attentively waiting for me to signal him that I had the package and that the merchandise was complete. Suddenly, I saw two cars approaching with some guys who had half their bodies out of the windows. They were carrying revolvers in their hands. They started shooting at the man. He fell to the ground. I ducked in my car and lifted my head slightly to see what was happening. I saw they stopped and got out of a car, two guys approached, and they kept shooting at him. Then they got into their car and sped away. I saw that and immediately took off and didn't stop until I reached Pottstown.

"I had never witnessed a crime! And worse under those conditions! I don't know why they did that. I was saved! If I had started chatting with him, as I always did, it would have been me too!" I arrived in Pottstown and went straight to sleep for a while. I woke up at eight in the morning. I decided to deliver the merchandise to the 'Don' immediately.

"I'll only deliver four packages. After all, that man is dead, and he won't know if I got five or just four packages."

I knocked for quite a while and they didn't open, which seemed strange to me. I waited longer, and after ten minutes, the door opened. It was the 'Don' who opened it for me.

"How are you? Aren't your workers here today?" I asked.

"Today I gave them the day off," he replied. "I want to be calm, you know how this business is. Sometimes you need to be alone."

"Yes, it's true!" I responded. "It is necessary on some occasions."

"How did it go?" he asked me. "Come, let's go to the study."

"This is the package that man gave me," I said and handed him the package.

"But, there are only four. He should have given you five," he said, puzzled.

"Look, I think you were lucky," I told him. "Because I think they killed that man when he was going to give me the last package."

"And what happened?" he asked me very surprised

"I arrived at the place where you sent me," I said to him. "I parked the car halfway down the block. I went to look for the man and he appeared right away. He started talking to him and suddenly his phone rang and he told me to wait because he wanted to know who was calling. He started talking and suddenly his voice rose. And he ended up arguing with someone, I don't know who. I realized he was being threatened, I think, based on what I heard him answer. He turned off the phone and very angrily said to me: 'These people think they're the best.' I replied: 'And what happened?' Then he said he didn't like being threatened, especially when he was going to leave them well.

"After that, he told me where the four packages were. 'While you look for those packages, I'll go for one that I'm missing.' I asked him if he would take long and he said no, he would be back quickly. I went to where the packages were, took them, opened the car door, and put them inside. When I was going to leave to let him know everything was fine, I looked in the rearview mirror to see if the man was there to see my signal. However, what I saw were two cars approaching quickly, with people halfway out of the car. When they got closer, I noticed they had guns. The first thing that occurred to me was to stay inside the car and wait to see what would happen. But I never imagined they would shoot the man. He tried to get into his house, but it seems a bullet hit him in the back as he tried. Then he fell to the ground and the cars stopped. Those men got out and went to finish him off. And when they were sure, they got into their cars and left at full speed. I, seeing that, sank into the seat until they disappeared. Then I started the car and came here."

"Well, it's true that I was saved. Because if they killed him," he told me, "I don't have to pay him. And you, you got twice what I offered you, because all the money is for us!" He paid me and I went home. That day, I decided to retire from that business. So I just kept the money and did some things at home and around noon, I headed back to Don's house to inform him of my decision to retire.

That day I parked my car a street away from his house and from there I saw several patrol cars and three detective cars, as well as an ambulance. There were many people watching what had happened. I got out of the car and leaned on it to see which house had the problem. I saw it was Don's house. Then I thought they had discovered him.

"I hope he doesn't say that I brought the merchandise. It seems they are going to take him out in handcuffs and with bodyguards. And today, his helpers aren't here! Today he gave them the day off. Precisely, today he was alone. What bad luck! But he won't say anything about me. Because I don't sell drugs, I just bring them. I don't think he will say anything. I trust him, and he trusts me," I continued watching from afar what was happening. The paramedics came out with a body on the stretcher. Five minutes later, the police came out with Don's wife detained. She was like crazy and had her hands and clothes covered in blood. She was screaming very loudly!

"If he's not for me, he won't be for anyone!"

"What could have happened at Don's house, precisely today when he was alone? Did Don hit his wife? Why is she soaked in blood and acting crazy?"

I got a bit closer and people were crowding around trying to see what had happened.

"Did you see, young man?" an old lady beside me said.

"Yes, I saw the girl that the police put in the car," I replied trying to play it cool.

"Yes, look at her! She's like crazy," she answered.

"What happened there?" I asked trying to find out.

"Oh, son, if you only knew," she replied, "it seems the girl found her husband in bed with another woman and then the devil possessed her and she stabbed him to death. Then she called the police, and she's all covered in blood because she stabbed herself multiple times. Her kids were crying desperately and I thought of peeking in because the door was open and I saw a lot of blood everywhere. The police arrived immediately. Look, you better not investigate and don't get too close."

I listened to the lady and left. "Now I really have to retire and for good. Because if I stay in this, the next victim will be me. Now I have the opportunity, and I have to take it."

Before getting into the car, I looked back at the house one last time.

"May God take you for a good rest and have you in His glory, my friend." I never knew his name, nor was I interested in knowing it because we only saw each other once or twice a month.

I got home and twenty minutes later my uncle arrived to talk to me.

"Ronaldito, you worked for Don, didn't you?" he asked trying to find out.

"No, actually I just did a few trips for him," I replied.

"Well, you sure kept that to yourself," he said.

"No, I already told you, man, it was just a couple of times," I said.

"Hey, why don't you lend me a few bucks?" he said to me, "to buy some material, and then I can invest it and get double back and I'll be able to pay you."

"Look, uncle, you don't know what I've been through," I replied, "to save some money. And you want me to lend it to you. I can't do it. But I can sell you some cheap material."

"Fine, nephew," he replied happily, patting me on the back like I was his favorite nephew. After I gave him the material, he treated me as if I had done something wrong to him. He was always angry and responded very badly when I talked to him. He made a face at Lorena. So we decided to move out of there. When I told him about my decision to leave, he got even angrier and argued with me because he didn't want us to go since I was paying them rent. In the end, we left. Since then, my uncle never paid me what he owed me and I never collected on him. Later on, Lorena took me to meet her mom and stepdad, who by the way seemed like nice people, but they really loved gatherings to talk and criticize people.

Two years later, my uncle Gregorio's girlfriend called me to say that my uncle had died from an asthma attack.

"Ronaldito!" she said to me on the phone. "With this problem, I don't have money for the funeral, it's very expensive. I need ten thousand dollars!"

"Look, call me later while I try to get it," I replied. But she never called me back and then I realized she was lying to me. The same week she called me, the police came to my house to ask about my uncle.

"Who's at the door?" asked my wife.

"The police, ma'am," they replied.

My wife opened the door and I came over to see what they wanted.

"Are you Mr. Castillo?" the policeman asked me.

"Yes, I am," I replied surprised, since I didn't have any problems with the police.

The officer kept looking at a photograph he had in his right hand.

"What's going on?" I asked doubtfully. "I don't have any problems with you."

The policeman with the photograph asked his partner.

"It's not him," he said. "He doesn't look like this," he said, showing him the photo.

"Doesn't matter. Look, they're relatives," replied the other sarcastically.

Even knowing it wasn't me, they took me anyway and I didn't know anything. Once at the station, they asked me about my uncle. Then I told them what his girlfriend had told me on the phone.

"Look, officer, his girlfriend called me and said my uncle died and she didn't tell me when or where because she immediately hung up on me."

"But do you know where he lives?" he asked.

"No. He never told me," I replied.

The moment they were questioning me, another policeman arrived and said my wife had called saying she was in labor.

"Young man, is your wife pregnant?" the policeman asked me.

"Yes, why?" I replied surprised.

"Well, she just called and says she's having labor pains," he replied. "So we're going to let you go, but if what you told us about your uncle is a lie, we'll come for you at your house and arrest you."

"But I have no way to get home," I told them. "You brought me here and I think you should take me back."

"There's no one to take you," he answered laughing. "If you're in a hurry, do it yourself."

"I'm not moving from here!" I told them. "And if something happens to my wife, be prepared for the consequences, because it was you who brought me!"

In the end, they took me home, and Lorena told me that the labor pains weren't true, that she only said it to get them to leave me alone.

A couple of months later my son was born and for me, it was a great happiness. Two years later my daughter was born, who became the pride of the family for being the first granddaughter. Those days we celebrated my son's birthday and Lorena's brothers, sisters, and parents attended.

"Hey, Ronaldito! I want to talk to you," said Lorena's brother Polito to me. "Now, because it's urgent!"

"About what, Polito?" I asked curiously. "What's so urgent?"

"Look, Rolando, I need you to give me a job," he replied lowering his voice. "You know, I want to sell drugs for you."

"Hey! Shh! Polito," I replied trying to make sure no one heard. "We'll talk about it tomorrow. It's not possible today. You know!"

"Fine, I'll come tomorrow," he responded.

The party ended at dawn and at six on the dot, Polito was knocking on my door.

"Hey, Polito! Why are you here at this hour?" I shouted angrily. "It's six in the morning! And I just went to bed!"

"Forgive me, Rolando, but it's urgent," he said desperately.

I got dressed and we went for a walk. We talked about the business and I decided to give him a little help. He started selling drugs little by little. We were like that for two months and he was good with the money. But, after that time, he started failing me; he didn't give me the full amount of money and he didn’t meet the deadlines he set. I kept giving him opportunities; however, he didn’t respond. One day, my daughter got sick, and I had to take her to the hospital.

"Rolando, Rolando!" my wife shouted desperately. "Come quickly, the girl is unwell, I don't know what's wrong with her!"

"What's wrong with the girl?" I asked, frightened.

"I don't know. She fainted!" she told me trembling.

I took my daughter in my arms and took her to a doctor. My wife dressed my son, closed the door, and arrived later at the hospital.

Polito was spying on us without us knowing and took advantage of the moment to enter my apartment and took the little "material" I had and ten thousand dollars in cash that I kept in case of an emergency.

"Lorena, did you leave the apartment open or what?" I said surprised since the door was open.

"No, I closed it when I left," she replied puzzled.

"Well, look, the door was open," I replied as I entered.

I turned on the light and saw that the glass on the entrance door was broken.

"It looks like someone broke in!"

"How?" she replied in horror.

"Yes! Look, the glass is broken," I got closer to check the crystal. "But don't worry, because I will find out tomorrow."

I knew someone would tell me who it was.

And they did. The next day, I met the old man who cleaned the building.

"Good morning, Jaimito!" I greeted the man. "How are you this morning?"

"Good, young man," he replied, with a big smile.

"Jaimito, sorry for the trouble, did anyone come to visit us yesterday? Didn't you see anyone?"

"Yesterday? At what time, young man?" the man replied trying to remember.

"Between twelve in the afternoon and two in the afternoon," I said hoping he would remember.

"Ah! I remember now. The only one I saw was Polito, your brother-in-law," he replied calmly. "He was knocking on your apartment door. Since he always comes, I didn't say anything. He knocked three times at your house door and I didn't see more because I was at the street entrance talking with a friend. But... I didn't see him leave. Weren't you there?"

"No. That's why I'm asking, because a glass on the door is broken, and I'm missing some money," I said worriedly. "But the money is not the important part, it's the abuse of confidence from this young man."

"Talk to him," he said. "Maybe it wasn't him."

I got so upset that I immediately went looking for him. I didn't find him anywhere.

Ten days after the incident, I saw him coming down the street and waited for him. It annoyed me that the closer he got to where I was, the more he laughed.

"Hey! What happened?" I asked him. "I heard you were the one who broke into my house to steal! And you disappeared to avoid explaining! And now that I see you, you laugh like what you did was funny!"

"The problem was," he replied laughing cynically, "that I owed money and they wanted to kill me, so I came to your house in an emergency to ask you for a loan and since you weren't there... you know, I had to hide here so they wouldn't catch me. Then I remembered you had some 'material' and I took it to pay those people off. That's the only way I got them off my back."

"But that's not right! Because I also have many responsibilities with your sister, with your nephews and with the guys working for me. And I trusted you, and look what you do to me!"

"But brother-in-law, I had to do it to save my life," he replied with a big smile. "I will pay you back later. When I get the money," he said in a more serious tone.

"I no longer trust you!" I said very angry. "Because what you did is an abuse of trust. And you still owe me the overdue payments, you know? You only have a week!"

I went into my house and Lorena noticed the argument between her brother and me.

"Rolando, what's happening? Because I saw you arguing with my brother and that's not okay," Lorena said to me.

"What's happening is that he stole the money I had saved to pay the workers. And now I will pay them late, and maybe they won't want to work with me until I pay them. All because of your little brother!"

I didn't tell her the whole truth because I didn't want her to find out that I was involved with drugs.

"I will talk to him," she said. "As soon as I see him."

Three weeks passed and we heard nothing from him. I was planning on how to collect the money he owed me. I decided to buy an iron bar and wrap it with black electrical tape and then wait near his house since he would eventually come, and then give him a few hits without breaking his bones.

Because then I would call the police and I would end up losing. I thought about all that for three days. I then decided to go to a bar that was near my house.

"Rolando! How are you, buddy?" an old friend said to me. "Come, sit here with me! I'll buy you a beer!"

"How are you, Don José? Thanks for the beer."

We chatted for a while, and I told him about the theft Polito committed at my house.

"Look, boy," Don José said, "your 'brother-in-law' is an addict, did you know? And he's always getting into trouble! But what he did to you is not right. Tell me, how can one steal from their own family? Especially when the family is always helping!"

"That's right! Now I don't know where he is," I told him. "But the day I see him, I'm going to beat him up."

"Look! Who's walking in here?" he said, bowing his head a little and speaking softly.

I turned and saw Polito. I got up quickly and went toward him. I took him by the arm and said:

"Let's go outside, I need to talk to you right now."

He stared at me and tried to be brave. He tried to shake me off, but I didn't give him a chance. We headed to a closed street next to the bar.

"Where's my money? Or tell me when you're going to give it to me," I said angrily. "Because I'm not playing!"

He started laughing at me because he saw I said it politely. Then his attitude made me so angry that I lifted him and threw him to the ground. I had the habit of carrying a knife with me, and I was so mad that I was about to stab him in the neck, but suddenly Don José appeared.

"You can't do that," he said, grabbing the hand that held the knife. "Because it's not worth ruining your life over this bad addict and thief."

When he let go of my hand, I beat Polito until I got tired. Then he got up and ran away. I went home and spent the whole afternoon with my kids watching TV. In the evening, there was a knock on the door, and the mother of my children went to answer it.

"Hi, Quique," she greeted her other brother. "What's going on?"

"Where's Rolando?" the brother asked. "Where is Rolando? Because we came to settle a matter with him!"

"What's happening? Why are you so upset?" Lorena asked him.

"It turns out Rolando hit Polito for no reason, and look how he left him," he pointed outside, where Polito waited all beaten.

Lorena peeked outside and saw him.

"Rolando! Rolando! Come here!" she yelled angrily.

"What's going on, woman? Why all the shouting?"

"Why didn't you tell me what you did to my poor brother?" she said desperately. "Look how you left him!"

"Because those are not your problems," I replied angrily. Outside, the brothers shouted insults at me.

"Come out if you're a man! Because right now, you and I are going to see if you act like such a big man with me. Come out!" shouted Polito's younger brother.

I grabbed a machete I had there and decided to confront them both. Lorena stood in the door and stopped me. Her mom and stepdad arrived at that moment, and when the lady saw the machete I was carrying, she desperately pleaded with me not to harm her sons.

"No, Ronald! Please, don't go out!" she yelled, kneeling. "Don't do anything to my sons! They are not bad! Sometimes they just get carried away. They are young! You know how they are!"

"Look, ma'am, don't tell me they are young!" I replied. "You know Polito is already thirty! And Quique is my age! So don't come at me with that! The worst thing is that he came to steal from me because he's an addict!"

"No! He's not an addict," she replied quickly. "Sometimes he drinks beer, but he doesn't use drugs. Where did you get such a lie?"

"It's not a lie, ask him," I responded confidently.

His mom convinced me not to go fight her sons. I then tried to talk to Quique and explain how things happened. He was so angry that he didn't want to listen, and I decided to lock myself in my room to calm down.

Lorena convinced her brother to listen and explained more or less what the problem was. I found out later that Polito disrespected his mom, and Quique had to hit him to stop him from offending her.

I woke up early and went for a walk. I went to a river near my house. The trees were already losing their leaves, which lay on the grass forming a brown and orange carpet. There was a very comfortable breeze, and the river water ran silently and peacefully. I walked for maybe two hours trying to clear my mind because I was still angry with my wife's family and even with her. I returned at noon, and Lorena was waiting for me at the door.

"I want an explanation about yesterday's problem with my brothers," she told me. "Because I already know what it’s about. And I know my brother might be whatever, but he was going to pay you!"

"What do you want me to say?" I replied disdainfully. "That I gave your brother what he deserved and I feel really good about it! And that I'm going to keep waiting for my money! It doesn't matter how I get it! It's my money, period!"

"But I know it's from drugs!" she replied, upset. "And you can have it whenever you want and my brother can't! Besides, my brother only borrowed it, and I think you have to forgive him, because it's easier for you to get it!"

"No! He stole it from me! It wasn't borrowed because he didn't ask me! And you know I'm right!" I replied shouting, because I was angry at the way she defended him. As if he really were innocent. And not because of giving him so much trust does he have the right to abuse it like that.

"But you have more money!" she said. "What he took is nothing compared to what you have!"

"So you believe I'm rich and have a lot of money, don't you?" I said incredulously. "But even if that were true, that money would be to buy a house for the kids and us," I replied. "Because I don't want to keep renting as until now!"

Once I told her that, she calmed down and didn't say anything else. I had no choice but to take out my money because, as she already knew, she was always asking me for various things. Like to buy herself a new car.

"Rolando, I need you to give me money," she told me that day.

"How much do you want?" I asked.

"About twenty thousand dollars!" she replied very calmly.

"And why do you want so much money, woman?" I asked doubtfully.

"I need a new car, because I'm embarrassed for my friends to see me in that old car," she said somewhat alarmed.

"Look, woman, it's fine that I have my little savings," I replied, "but we're not rich."

"I know!" she answered. "That's why I'm asking you for a cheap car. Besides, I'm your wife, and I believe it's your obligation to give me everything I need."

"Fine, we'll buy it this weekend," I preferred to buy it for her to avoid more problems than I had when I hit her brother. Because she changed from that day on. She got upset about everything.

That weekend we went to buy her car. She picked it out, and incidentally, she changed it two months later for a more current one, supposedly because something was wrong with the engine. I know it was easy to fix. Five months later, she asked me again to buy her a new one.

"Woman! Why do you want a new car?" I asked desperately. "You've only had this one for five months!"

"It's just that I left it parked and I don't know who scratched it," she said very authoritatively. "And now I don't like it anymore!"

"But that scratch can be fixed!" I replied.

"No! Because it's not the same. I want it pristine!" she told me.

I accepted all that because I thought she loved me. She met some friends with whom she went to play cards, and she asked me for more money every day: for the gold necklace, the ring, the dress, the coat, the shoes, etc. But all at a very high price. So I decided to immediately look for a house before she finished blowing through the money.

I got approved for the credit. So I made the down payment, and the monthly payments were five hundred dollars. Some time ago, I had decided to slowly drift away from that bad business. Even though two months earlier I had the chance to meet a man who was already very wealthy and wanted me to help with his businesses. That is, to deliver and pick up packages in New York and collect the money he was paid at locations. We became good friends, and he started going to Postín. I trusted him a lot and let him stay the night at the house, since as he still didn't know the town well, it was preferable for him to stay in a safer place.

"Rubén! Stay at my house, you know my house is yours too. You can leave whenever you want tomorrow!" I would tell him with a lot of confidence, since he was Cuban just like me.

15
THE BETRAYAL

Winter came. One night when it was too cold, I dropped off the guys who worked for me at their homes, and I headed to mine. I went in, and Lorena was watching TV.

"Hey! Good that you're back, Rolando!" Lorena shouted from the living room. "Come here for a moment!"

"What's up, woman? Greet me first," I replied, surprised.

"I want you to go to the store," she told me. "Because I don't have cigarettes, and I would like to eat a sandwich too."

"But woman! Why didn't you go earlier?" I replied, annoyed by the time. "Besides, you know I come home very tired from work!"

"Come on! Why don't you want to go?" she replied. "Don't you say you love me a lot! Show it by pleasing me!"

The woman insisted so much that she convinced me and I went. I took my bicycle, which was completely new, since I hadn't used it due to lack of time. In ten minutes I arrived at the restaurant. I left the bicycle leaning against the entrance to keep an eye on it.

"Ma'am, I want two sandwiches and some cigarettes. Please wait," I said to the lady, seeing that a boy about my age was grabbing my bicycle and already putting his foot on it. "Let me see what that boy wants with my bicycle!"

"Is that all?" she told me as she leaned over to see what was happening.

"Yes! I'll be right back!" I answered and went out.

"It's nice, isn't it?" I asked the boy. "If you're interested, we can come to an arrangement."

"Why are you asking me that?" he replied.

"Because I see you're checking it out," I told him. "And that bicycle is mine."

"And why do I care it's yours?" he said mockingly. I tried to take my bicycle from where he had put it. I ignored what he said to avoid problems.

I already had enough with the trouble caused by Lorena's brother.

"Where are you going with that bike, jerk?" the boy said as he stepped in front of me. Since I'm not Boricua, the bad word didn't offend me, so I ignored him.

"Let me pass, I don't want trouble with you," I said courteously. "Don't bother me!"

I saw a boy approach and I turned to look at him. I realized I knew him. He was a Boricua named Roberto.

"Hey, dude, leave the Cuban alone!" Roberto told the guy who was bothering me.

"Don't get involved," the other said, pushing him.

"Look, don't mess with him because you don't know what surprise he might have for you," replied Roberto. "Because those are the dangerous ones! Let's get to the car and stop fooling around!"

He took him by the arm and then another man came over and helped him get to the car. Meanwhile, I put my bicycle back at the restaurant entrance. I went in to pick up what I ordered and Roberto caught up with me.

"Look 'Cuba', sorry for that fool," he told me. "But he's like that because he's drunk."

"Well, not that drunk!" I said. "Because he knows well what he's telling me."

"Yeah, I know," he replied. "Actually, with four beers he drinks, he gets like that."

"What is that man to you?" I asked, puzzled.

"He's my brother-in-law," he answered with a gesture of resignation.

"Well, I don't want problems with anyone," I said worriedly because I turned and the guy was already on my bicycle. "Look what your brother-in-law is doing! I want to avoid a problem!"

"What's wrong with that idiot!" he exclaimed upon seeing him.

I put my food in a backpack I was carrying and slung it over my shoulder. We headed to the door.

"Hey, dude! Leave that bicycle alone," Roberto was telling him. "Let's go to the car."

He took him by the arm and another guy who was with him ran to grab him from the other side. The guy started struggling to break free. I noticed he had a beer bottle in his hand and wouldn't let it go despite the effort he made to escape the other two guys. I climbed on my bicycle and was getting ready to leave when I felt a blow on my right eyebrow. I turned to see who hit me and then I felt another strong blow on my left eyebrow. I let go of the bike and fell to the ground. In front of me, I saw some feet. I pulled hard on them. I was very dizzy and couldn't clearly see the person who fell. I went up to them because I assumed it was the person who had hit me. Then I found myself facing the "dude." We started struggling and I drew a knife I always kept hidden. I was so angry that I stabbed him two or three times in the back and then he let go of me.

"He's got a knife!" he screamed desperately. "He's got a knife because he pricked me!"

He had a piece of bottle in his hand and wanted to cut me. I was quicker and stopped his hands. I couldn't hold back and stabbed him in that hand again. As his friends saw he didn't get up, they ran to see what was happening. Meanwhile, I went straight home. I arrived and gave the things to my wife and headed to the bathroom.

"What's wrong with you! You don't even look at me!" the mother of my children was saying as she followed me to the bathroom.

"See! That's why I didn't want to go anywhere," I answered and locked the bathroom door.

I took off the balaclava I had worn to go out since it was winter and very cold. I looked at myself in the mirror and was scared to see two big wounds on each eyebrow. I couldn't believe it. I was covered in blood. I suddenly remembered my mother's home remedies and asked my wife for sugar. Not even sugar managed to stop the bleeding.

"But look how you've got those wounds," Lorena said scared. "What happened? What did you do?"

"I didn't do anything!" I said angrily.

"Let's go to the hospital! Because you need stitches," she said nervously.

"I don't want to go because they're going to ask me what happened and I'm not going to tell them the truth," I replied.

"They're not going to ask you anything. Let's go!" she said.

She convinced me and we went to the emergency room. We left my children under their grandmother's care.

"If they ask what happened, tell them I fell off the bike. Don't tell them anything else! Is that okay?" I said to her.

"Don't worry, I won't say anything," she replied.

I went into an examination room and was attended to by a nurse.

"What happened to you?" she asked.

"I fell off the bike," I replied.

"How was the fall? Because the bruises are on the sides," the nurse said.

"I don't know," I replied. "Because it all happened so fast!"

While I was waiting for the doctor to stitch me up, I saw that Lorena was being questioned by some police officers. She was pointing towards where I was, and I felt like running away from there. The doctor was cleaning my wounds to start stitching me. Meanwhile, the mother of my children got up and came over to where I was.

"Can I talk to Rolando for a moment?" Lorena asked the doctor.

"No. Wait a moment. If you want, you can wait in here," the doctor said. "When I'm done, talk to him."

"I'll be back in a moment," the doctor said as he got up. "I'm out of anesthesia!"

I took the opportunity to talk to Lorena.

"What were the police asking you?" I said to her.

"It's just that they were going to put me in jail," she stammered. "For being an accessory and I had to tell them the truth."

I felt so bad when she told me that I thought: "If she knows I'm not a troublemaker and that I want to avoid problems! Because with her brother's problem, I have enough! How could she think of telling the police the truth! I'm a fool for believing she loves me! Even though I know she changed so much after finding out I have money. And I go out of my way to please her in everything to make her happy, and look what she does for me! I don't know how I let her convince me to go get what she wanted from the store, if she had plenty of time during the day to go herself! Look at the trouble I'm in! It seems she's happy while I'm in these situations! If they put me in jail, she'll be happier than ever!"

"Forgive me, I got nervous!" she said to me. "I didn't mean to!"

The doctor finished and immediately the police approached and started asking me questions about a problem that occurred on the street.

"We were called because someone stabbed a man several times," they said. "And we got a description that looks like you! We came to ask you what happened at that restaurant."

"Well, I don't know anything about that!" I replied while turning to look at the mother of my children with great anger. "Because what happened to me," I said, touching the wounds on my eyebrows, "is because my bike slipped on the ice, and I fell, hitting the curb!"

"Look, you have to come with us," they said as they took my hands and put the handcuffs on me. "Because what you're saying isn't very convincing, and this isn't the right place for an investigation. So, we'll take you to the police station."

I tried to convince them, but they didn't believe me. They put me in the police car, and inside I heard them talking to Lorena.

"Look, don't worry, we're not taking you," they said. "Everything will be fine, he will tell us."

At the station, a detective asked me questions about what happened, and I maintained that I hadn't done anything. The detective played a taped cassette where my wife explained the events step by step; from that moment, I began to hate her voice. I had no choice but to tell them how the problem went down.

"What we're interested in," said a police officer, "is knowing who had the weapon."

"The other guy had the knife," I replied, "and when we were struggling, I managed to take it from him and stabbed him with it. Moreover, I acted that way because he was with three other guys."

Three hours later they let me go and I walked home. The ground was slippery with the melting snow, but with the cold, it became ice. I thought about many things on the way. "Rolando, you're an idiot! Why do you help people when they always repay you with hypocrisy and betrayal? Look at what your wife did! What would it have cost her to say she didn't know about this matter? But it's your fault for trusting her!" Sometimes I laughed, sometimes I wanted to scream. "Change towards everyone! Do you see what Polito did to you for being nice to him? And still, your wife turned against you. She changed towards you... she started demanding money. And you, just to make her happy, are putting your hands in the fire. And she, far from thanking you... on the contrary, demands more and now treats you like a dog. All of this is because... she doesn't love you. She's with you because she knows you give her what she wants. She doesn't care how you get it! She doesn't care if one day you'll get killed! But you, just to keep thinking she loves you, do everything, Rolando... even if it hurts to accept she doesn't love you." At that moment I came back from my thoughts and saw that I was walking slowly down the street and I no longer cared about the cold or the annoying snow where my feet were sinking. I felt the tears rolling down my cheeks. "I'm crying like a child when he loses the most valuable thing in his life! But I... don't know what I've lost. Because she's not what I expected. I love my children! But... it hurts to have given everything, renouncing my dignity as a human being. To have loved knowing it wasn't reciprocated!... I think... now I know what I lost. My own worth! Because I was a coward for not accepting it before. Now she has me in her hands because she knows how I get the money. I'm going to treat her as if nothing happened, because if I don't, she's capable of betraying me again!"

I got home and acted as if nothing had happened.

"What did the guards ask you?" she questioned nervously.

"Nothing, they just told me to tell them how the accident I had happened," I replied as if it was nothing, since I didn't want her to find out anything. Why be so legal with her if she wasn't with me?

I continued fulfilling her whims, as always. I felt obligated to do it, I felt trapped. All because I trusted her with how I got my money!

Since I had a little cocaine, I went to sell it and used it as an excuse to be out of the house, because I couldn't stand her being near me. Some days I stayed in a room rented by an old lady, and other days I stayed in a hotel. At home, I tried to be there as little as possible.

My small business started to decline and the guys were looking for me everywhere until they found me. I fell into a depression to the point that nothing mattered to me. I started inhaling cocaine and at the same time smoking a marijuana cigarette; then I felt happy and went out to meet girls to forget the problems. I was like this for almost two months, and one day when I was leaving the house I was renting, Polito was passing by with his wife.

"What cowards we are when we get married!" he shouted loudly for me to hear.

I got upset and went back inside the house. I looked for an aluminum tube I had stored and put it in another one I had on the bike behind the seat. I went out again. I approached where Polito was.

"What happened to my money, Polito?" At that moment I saw that his wife was about five meters away from us, taking care of her baby in a stroller.

"You're not going to collect anything from me," he shouted at me angrily. "What are you up to with my dear sister?" he asked demandingly.

I didn't answer him, I turned around and went for the tube I had put on the bike. I took it out and started hitting him. His wife saw the fight and then left the child on the pavement and went to defend her husband. Later I found out from a friend that the wife had taken her baby out of the stroller and when she saw us fighting, she threw her on the ground and the baby started crying.

The lady wanted to hit me and I pushed her aside. I gave her a beating and left the place. The next day some policemen came to my house to look for me. It was all because Polito's wife filed a complaint against me, accusing me of hitting her one-month-old baby. According to the summons, I had to appear before a person representing Polito and his wife.

I felt like going for him and beating him with sticks again. That way they would put me in jail for a good criminal case, and I no longer cared about life.

Lorena also started going out with her mother to dance and drink at bars, coming back in the early morning. Her mother, instead of advising her, invited her.

One afternoon I got home and found my three children alone (my third child is her son, but since I practically raised him, I say he's mine).

"Where is your mom?" I asked my eldest son.

"She went out with my grandma," he answered hesitantly. "I don't know where they went."

"Have you eaten?" I asked, because it was already seven in the evening and I didn't see anything prepared in the kitchen.

"We haven't eaten, because my mom said she would make us something when she gets back," he replied. "And we are very hungry!"

"How can it be possible that this woman left the kids alone to go out with her mom and also left them without eating!"

The four of us had dinner and later there was a knock on the door. I opened it and saw it was a friend of hers and mine.

"Rolando! How are you?" he greeted me a bit nervously.

"Fine Javier, come in," I said, stepping aside to let him in. "What brings you here?"

"Well, I... well, I just came to check that the kids were okay," he said, rubbing his hands. "It's good that you check them!"

"Do you know where Lorena is?" I asked curiously.

"Well yes, she's at the bar with her mom," he replied. "But don't tell her I told you where to find her."

"Don't worry," I said. "Look, can you do me a favor?"

"Yes, tell me what you want me to do," he said very enthusiastically.

"Watch over my kids for a moment," I said as I put on my coat. "I'm going to the bar to see this woman."

"Alright," he said, getting closer to me. "Don't be rash," he said, putting a hand on my shoulder.

"Don't worry, I won't do anything," I said smiling. "I'm not a fool!"

I went in and saw her sitting at a table, accompanied by her mom and two guys. She was laughing loudly. I walked and stood in front of her so she would see me.

"Rolando!" I heard her shout, but I already ignored her and left that place.

"Mmm, one of the men with whom Lorena was is Rubén! What is she doing with him? I don't know the other one, but it seems this woman's sea is dead for him. How big that woman is!"

I arrived home and Javier was already desperate.

"Good thing you came, Rolando!" he said as he stood up. "Because I have a matter to resolve! See you soon!"

"Take care," I replied. "Take care, gently."

As soon as he left, I went to shower and lay down with my kids.

I didn't care what time their mother would arrive. It was almost dawn when the noise at the bedroom door woke me up. I lifted my head and opened one eye to see who it was. At the threshold, I saw Lorena standing with a stick in her hand. She walked towards me.

"Didn't Javier tell you that I went out with my mom?" she said to me not very clearly because she was already tipsy.

"Yes, he told me," I replied. "But someone else told me where you were."

"And who was it?" she asked very annoyed.

"Don't worry," I responded. "If until now you didn't care if your kids eat or not. With that you told them you'd come back to make them something. But since the bar and the little cubans were better, you preferred to stay there. Isn't that true?"

She didn't like what I said and wanted to hit me with the stick she was carrying. I stepped aside and took it away from her. I hit her on the leg with the same stick, leaving a mark. I went back to sleep since the next day I had to get up really early to work.

It dawned snowing and I had to go with the guys to do a really big job, therefore there was a lot of money involved. "I have to let the guys know we won't be working. The weather is really bad and we won't be able to do anything."

It was seven in the morning and I hadn't slept well because of the problem with my wife at dawn. I arrived at Juan's house, one of the guys who worked for me.

"Juan, I just wanted to let you know that today we won't be able to work. Because look how it's snowing and this snow won't let us work," I commented. "Tell the others I'll let them know when we'll start."

"Alright, Rolando," he answered resignedly. "I'll tell them."

Before getting home, I touched my pockets and saw I didn't have the keys to enter. I found it strange because I never forgot them. I had no other choice but to knock on the door.

"Why won't they open for me? Could it be that this woman is still asleep?" I looked at my watch and saw it was nine in the morning. "It can't be that she is still asleep, because the kids won't let her sleep. I'll take a look to see if they hear me from there." As I went down the hallway that led to the back of the house, I approached the bathroom window and heard the shower was on and there was a smell of conversation, but not clearly. I went to the kids' room window and knocked on it. Emilio, the eldest, peeked out.

"Son, open the door for me," I said.

I followed the hallway back and remembered that I always left a window half open for emergencies. No one knew, not even Lorena. I opened it and entered. Then I saw Lorena coming out of the bathroom. When she saw me, she was stunned. I approached and saw that my "friend" Rubén was in the bathroom. I understood what was happening. Meanwhile, she went to the bedroom, and I followed her.

"Why did you do this to me?" I shouted at her. "And with someone you claimed to be my friend! How many times have you been with him, and I let him stay in my house!"

"Nothing really happened. We didn't do anything," she replied nervously and with a stammering voice.

"And what do you want me to think? If you come completely disheveled and he is bathing as if nothing happened! Besides, I heard you talking now that I came through the hallway. Tell me then why did you leave the children locked in the room so they wouldn't notice! Isn't that so? And why did you take the keys from my pocket? And with all that, you say you did nothing! I should kill both of you!"

I left the room and went to where "Rubén" was to kick him out of my house. I spent some time pondering the situation. "It's not worth dirtying my hands. If I do something to her, what will become of my children? And me in jail? No, that's not right!"

The snow stopped, and I went to work with the boys. My disappointment didn't let me be at peace. I couldn't believe it! It wasn't possible that I loved this woman so much who wasn't worth it! But that was the reality! I felt annihilated, undone, crushed. What was I going to do from that day on? I didn't know. I couldn't resign myself to being alone!

I loved my children, I love them, and I will always love them, but I never made them part of the problem between their mother and me. At that time, it pained me too much to leave them abandoned. That was another reason that held me back from continuing with their mother, besides loving her as I did. Maybe unconsciously, I used my children as an excuse to stay with her. What I am sure of is that I didn't want to be alone.

I was coming back from work around four thirty. In the street, Lorena's brother was waiting for me.

"Rolando, come on man!" he shouted instantly, raising his hand.

"What's up, Quique? What brings you here?" I greeted and approached him. "Why so mysterious?"

"Come with me because you're in big trouble with my sister," he told me and took me by the arm to take me somewhere else.

"In trouble? Why?" I asked, puzzled. "If I haven't done anything to your sister."

"Look, let's go and I'll explain on the way," Quique said. We went in my small truck. I was driving, but I felt completely disoriented.

"I know you're not going to like it, as I didn't like that my sister did this to you," he said angrily. "Quique, tell me what's happening. Stop saying so many things and tell me what I want to know," I told him in a desperate tone.

"I brought you with me," he said. "Because if the police see you a hundred feet near your house, they'll arrest you."

"They'll... arrest me? Why?" I replied angrily.

"Because my sister filed a complaint against you," he said worriedly. "She told them you threatened her with death, that you hit her and that it was all for nothing. That she feared for the lives of her children and her own because you wanted to kill her for nothing. That you were crazy and that she hadn't gone to them before for fear that you would do something to them. And the police believed her. So, she told them if she saw you near your house, to call them, and they would arrest you on the day of the trial."

"How is it possible that she did this to me?" I replied very angrily. "It's true that we fought today at dawn and that she was drunk and wanted to hit me with a stick. I took it away from her and, being so angry, I hit her with it on the leg. Understand, yesterday she went out to the bar with your mom and left my children alone and without food. After that, she thought of sending a friend to check if they were okay. Meanwhile, another person told me she was in that place, and I went to see if it was true. You know she was very happy having fun with some of my friends. Still, she wanted to hit me... it's not right."

"I didn't know that," Quique replied stunned. "She told me that she didn't know the reasons why you wanted to kill her."

"Listen to me carefully, Quique," I said desperately. "This morning, I left early to see the boys working with me and thought I'd come back and apologize for what I did to her leg. But what was my unpleasant surprise, that when I looked for my house keys in my pants, I didn't have them. Then I arrived and knocked, and they didn't open. The thing is, your sister was with the one who claimed to be my friend, bathing. And I saw her when she came out of the bathroom all wet, and the other stayed inside. Even so, she denied it to me."

"Is that true?" he responded incredulously and angrily. "Elia didn't tell me any of that. She only told me that you hate her and that she doesn't even know why. That you don't love her children and that none of them matter to you. Despite what she said to me, I did not agree with what she did to you. Because I know you and I know you are not like that. Look, if you want, you can stay at my house while they solve their problem."

"Why does she have to do all this to me? I am bad, but I was willing to forgive her everything because I love her. And I think I don't want to lose her. Although she is already more lost than anything. Now I am sure that she doesn't love me. She even got the police on me! With this, instead of solving things, she made them worse. I'm going to put a cross on her because for me she is already dead." I left her brother at his house. I wanted to be alone and went to buy cocaine and beers. I tried to get a revolver to finish off everyone who was bothering me, but I found nothing. Instead, I met a girl named Carmen Rosa. Thanks to her, I forgot about all my problems and everyone who was creating them for a while.

"Hello, how did you wake up?" Carmen Rosa asked me. "I hope you're better today."

"Well, I think so," I said, sitting down in a chair.

"You know something," she came close and stroked my hair. "I was crazy to have you with me."

"But... we just met!" I responded surprised. "How is it that you already wanted to be with me?"

"I saw you a few times with the mother of your children," she replied. "And about two months ago I saw her with a guy. I thought at that time that you and she were no longer together."

"Well, how did you see her?" I asked. "What did you imagine then?"

"Well, very close and having a beer," she told me. "They were looking into each other's eyes, and she laughed flirtatiously. Mmmh, now I understand her attitude when Rubén went to my house and stayed there," I said angrily. "Did you let him stay at your house!?" she said surprised. "Friends are treated at the door to outside!"

"Yes, I know, but... you know that I'm not like that," I told her. "I can't change."

"Okay," she replied resignedly. "Now tell me, what attitude did your wife have when that man arrived?"

"I noticed that they looked into each other's eyes," I said with sadness and anger. "And on one occasion, during lunchtime, she served him food first and with too much attention. And lastly to me, as if I were a pot."

"Look, let's leave that subject," she replied. "What I like is that you're with me, and that's what I wanted."

"But... I still love her," I told her desperately. "And it might be that we get back together because I know she loves me."

"What!? You think she loves you with what she did to you?" she asked astonished. "I don't know why you defend her so much. If she betrayed you in your own house and still dared to file a complaint against you. When she's the poisonous one!"

I felt very calm with her. According to what she told me, the same thing happened to her as to me. I was very grateful because she offered me her home since those who called themselves my friends turned their backs on me. They were supporting Rubén and helping him sell the drugs he brought from New York.

"Carmen Rosa, I've been here in your apartment for fifteen days now, and I need to know what's happening at my house," I said anxiously. "I sense something strange. I need you to go investigate."

"Well, as long as you don't leave here... I'll go," she replied very confidently.

Evening was falling and Carmen hadn't returned, I was a bit nervous. I heard the door open: it was her.

"What happened? What's the situation over there?" I asked desperately.

"I'll tell you what I found out, but don't get upset," she said while taking off her coat. "The individual with whom your wife is now enters the house and stays there. Honestly, he already feels as if he's the owner of the house and to make matters worse, he brought a friend who is the boyfriend of your wife's mother, and he also stays in your house."

"Is he a boyfriend of that woman?" I said surprised. "But she has her husband!"

"Oh, I forgot to tell you that they already separated," she said. "Precisely because the husband found out."

"But... tell me one thing," I said thoughtfully. "Are those guys going to stay living there?"

"As far as I know, only while they're here in town, because according to them they have a house in New York."

My anger and helplessness increased. It wasn't possible that they were already calm, having destroyed my dreams! My suffering was infinite. The worst part was that I had no family to support me, to advise me.

"Rolando, don't worry," Carmen Rosa told me. "Those who do

wrong, pay for it sooner or later, and the price is very high because it costs tears of blood."

That girl gave me much strength to move forward. I decided to move to a hotel, and she accompanied me that day.

"How did you sleep, Rolando?" my friend asked me with much affection. "I brought you something for breakfast."

"With what money did you buy this?" I asked, surprised, because I had not given her any money.

"I came prepared just in case," she said, laughing.

"You know I need..." I said very thoughtfully.

"What?" she asked, approaching the bed.

"Clothes. I've had the same clothes for days and I feel bad," I got out of bed and went to the window. "Do you want to buy some?" she asked me.

"No! I want you to do me a favor..." I said, sitting on the small sofa. "Go to my house, to ask Lorena for my clothes. I'll wait for you in the car."

"Well, let's go!" she said, grabbing her bag and coat.

We arrived in front of the house, and she went to knock on the door. From afar, I saw Lorena open it and they said something. Carmen Rosa returned to where I was.

"Rolando! It's not possible!" she told me, crying angrily. "That woman! Well, the mother of your children, is awful. She yelled a bunch of insults at me as soon as I told her I was there for your clothes. She said if you were such a man, you should come to get them yourself. I told her not to be so shameless, that she knew you couldn't because she filed a report with the police.

But she told me that wasn't true, that she wasn't capable of doing that to the father of her children... Look, Rolando, I think she says that to keep appearances, because she asked me if I was with you and I said no. And she replied not to play dumb because I was the reason you left her, and that your kids and she need you. But that sounded very false to me. Be careful because those women are like scorpions, they sting without being harmed."

"Look, Carmen Rosa, I think she told the truth," I was convinced that Lorena hadn't filed any report. "I was blind and didn't believe anyone because I know deep inside that she still loves me. I don't think she's that bad."

"Well, I don't know," she said, annoyed. "What I realized is that she's a hypocrite and you shouldn't trust her."

"Look... don't take it the wrong way, but..." I said softly, trying not to hurt her because she was supporting me in these moments when I needed someone, and also because I was crying and she encouraged me to overcome my pain. "I think I should go get my clothes. That way I can talk to her and she can tell me what she wants us to do to remedy this situation."

"Look... you do what you think you should do," she said sadly. "And whatever happens, I'll be here to support you."

"Alright, don't move from here," I said, very sure that Lorena would come back with me. "I thought she was going to apologize for betraying me, and I was willing to forgive her. I didn't care about anything. I'll be back and I'll tell you what we agree on."

"Alright. I'll wait here. I don't want you to get into any trouble."

She stayed thoughtful in the car. I arrived at my house and didn't even have time to knock. She opened the door.

"Hey, jerk! What do you think of yourself?" she said with a terribly foul mouth. "Why did you send that prostitute to my house? If you know I'm not going to give you any clothes."

"How dare you say that to me!" I replied with tremendous anger. "You were the one who betrayed me, and in my house. Because I'm the one who supports it! And your brother told me you reported me after what you did to me. And now you tell my friend that you didn't go to the police. Is it true that you didn't go to the police?" I asked, hoping for a no.

"It's not true, I didn't go to the police," she said very confidently. "If I betrayed you, so what? Rubén has money. He can give me what I want."

"I don't want to listen anymore. I came for my clothes," I said. "And I won't bother you ever again. What hurts me is my children. But I have the right to see them, right?"

"I don't want you to see them," she replied very authoritatively.

"Why not, if they are my children?" I said, trying to contain the anger I had.

"Because I feel like it," she said mockingly.

"Alright, you think I'm going to die with all this you're doing to me, right?" I said more calmly, seeing that she had a mocking gesture on her face. "But no. Because I know how to start anew."

When I said that, she stepped aside. I went straight to the room and collected all my clothes. I was leaving through the front door, and she was to one side.

"Well, you're leaving and saying you can start anew, right?" she said mockingly. "Well, you'll see I can destroy you and do whatever I want with you whenever I want."

"Why that hatred against me?" I said. "You were the one who failed. You destroyed this home."

"Because that's how I am when someone bores me," she replied. "And because I didn't like what you did to my brother. And because you were gone for two or three days from the house and came back as if nothing."

"But you didn't care. You were going out with the one who was supposedly my friend," I replied coldly. "And I didn't even know."

"I did it because you are not capable of making an effort to give me what I need," she said, laughing.

"Alright. Let's see if I learn not to help just anyone, because you never know what habits people have. Let's see if you find someone like me again. Because I'm sure if you stay with Rubén, he'll make you work. And everything he gives you, he'll charge you double. Not like me, who has been giving you even what you don't deserve," I said with a mocking smile, turned around, and left. On the street, the police were waiting for me, and Carmen Rosa was beside them. At the moment I thought she had informed on them because she didn't want me to have problems.

"What's your name? Who are you?" one of the two policemen waiting for me said.

"My name is Rolando," I answered.

"What are you doing here?" he said.

"I came to get my clothes," I stretched out my hands to show them the clothes.

"Ah! I've seen you a few times!" said the policeman. "Do you know why I'm going to arrest you?"

"No, I don't know," I replied puzzled.

"Because the lady who lives in this house called about ten minutes ago and said you're bothering her and hit her on the arm! And also, you already knew that you can't come closer than a hundred meters, because we have to arrest you until the day of your trial!"

"Well, I didn't know that!" I replied indignantly. "She told me it wasn't a problem, and that thing about hitting her arm isn't true! I came calmly just for my clothes!"

"Well, you'll tell that to the judge because we're just doing our job!" the policeman said. Hearing that, I was astonished since that woman assured me that she hadn't filed any complaint against me, and I thought she couldn't do that to me. I asked them to let me give the clothes to Carmen Rosa.

"Take my clothes and go to your apartment," I said to her. "I'll call you on the phone later."

They handcuffed me and put me in the patrol car. I turned to look at Lorena, and she started laughing and closed the door.

I spent three days in a dark cell. I was very hungry and they only fed me twice a day: a slice of cheese, a slice of ham, and two pieces of bread. One of those days I thought of saving one of my rations, and at night I heard noises; it was the mice feasting on my food. After three days, a guard came.

"Rolando! You're going to accompany me, so get ready," he said, visibly angry. "You're going to see the judge!"

"Sir, but I need to take a bath. How am I going to present myself before the judge looking this dirty? At least let me wash up!" I told him.

"Look, if you want to get out of this problem," the police was telling me very angrily, "get ready because I'm the one who's going to take you to the judge."

The guard returned, and I was ready. They handcuffed my hands and feet. They put me in a patrol bus that had only a very small window. I tried to peek to see if there was anyone I knew outside, but I couldn't see anything. I sat down and was getting settled when the bus stopped. The door opened, and the guard pulled me.

"Get down quickly!" he told me, but I couldn't get down fast because of the cuffs on my feet. "We don't have much time left!"

A guard there helped me down. I walked and saw that all the guards had high-caliber weapons.

We entered the courthouse and they transferred me to a cell where there were seven other guys.

"Why did they bring you here? Do you have a trial?" one asked me, leaning against the bars.

"Yes, I have a trial," I answered gloomily.

"Why are you here?" another asked me.

"Because my woman made a false accusation against me," I said angrily.

"You have nothing to worry about," said one with a carefree smile. "We are here for more serious crimes."

"Don't worry," said another one who came out from among them. "The one in trouble is me because they're going to sentence me for murder, and I think I'll never get out." He was a guy about nineteen years old, and he seemed quite happy about that crime.

"Rolando Castillo!" the guard shouted. "Let's go to trial!"

"Good luck, Cuban," said the guys I was with in the cell. "Don't worry, today you'll be on the street."

I reached the courtroom, and the policeman opened the door for me. The first face I saw was that of shameless Lorena. Upon seeing me, she started laughing as if I were very amusing to her.

"Sit on the left side," a guard told me. Lorena was sitting on the opposite side.

The judge arrived and immediately called her name. She got up and stood at a desk in front of the judge.

"Raise your right hand and swear if what you will answer is true. If you lie, you will be condemned," said the judge as she did everything he instructed. "By just raising her hand, she is already lying," I thought as I saw her so confident and making an innocent face. "I don't know what she will say against me, but now that I see what she really is, I know she's worse than a snake."

She lowered her hand and immediately the judge proceeded to question her.

"According to this complaint..." the judge paused to better read what the paper he held in his hand said. "That Rolando, the father of your children, has psychologically abused you since you've been together and that moreover, he used to hit you a lot, which is why you don't want him next to you. That you have always taken care that your children don't see the beatings he gives you."

"Yes, Your Honor," she replied very seriously.

"That he didn't give you money for food, and that he would arrive and assault you for not giving him food," said the judge. "What other charges do you want to make against this man?"

"That lately he was falsely accusing me of going with my mother to drink at a bar! And that's not true! I was going to find a job to feed my children," she said with incredible cynicism. "Also, the last beating he gave me was because he accused me of being with someone in my own house, and that's not true either! That day I was with my children, and I took them to their room to sleep. When I left, he started to beat me."

"I am concerned about my children because he mistreats them too much! And he really doesn't love them as their father; he sees them as strangers! And before he gives them a bad hit and kills one of them, I prefer he leaves us alone!"

"Do you have a house, car, furniture, etc.? Who of the two bought them?" the judge asked her.

"Between the two of us, because I worked to help him pay half! But... he has always threatened to leave me on the street! Because when you love someone, you trust them blindly! And I let this man put our assets in his name!"

She said countless things I did not expect, and the judge didn't even look at me, didn't ask me anything, and I was about to run and scream due to the anger and pain caused by all the lies that woman said. She spoke so confidently about everything she said that it seemed true. There came a moment when she started to cry, and she was backed by a lawyer, and I was alone.

"Rolando, what do you have to say about all this?" the judge asked me.

"Your Honor, this woman is lying," I told him. "I can prove it. About seeing her with a man, it's true, and she lives with him in my own house!"

All my efforts to defend myself were in vain. The judge dismissed all my accusations against her and took me as a liar and abuser.

"Look, sir..." the judge said to me. "The jury has ruled that you are guilty, and therefore, you are prohibited from approaching within one hundred feet of the house, and you are also forbidden from seeing your children," it hurt me so much not being allowed to see my children, as they were my life and I was very used to them. "By the ruling given by the judge, I knew everything had already been arranged. Perhaps by Lorena's lawyer. In case you break what this honorable court has established, you will be imprisoned, and things will get worse."

Hearing that, I could not hold back the tears out of anger and frustration.

They let me out, and I decided to disappear from that woman's life and never showed up around that house again.

I went to Carmen Rosa's apartment, and since she wasn't there, I waited for her at the entrance door. I felt tired and fell asleep. When she arrived, she woke me up.

"Rolando! Wake up! Let's go inside! Look at how you are, all dirty, and how badly you smell!"

"Yes, indeed," I replied. "They left me in a dark cell and didn't even let me bathe."

Carmen Rosa was good to me, supporting me to move forward and not get depressed. We decided to live together and coordinated very well. I sold the construction business I had to one of the guys who worked with me, for eighteen thousand dollars, which he was paying me little by little.

The first ten thousand dollars I saved without telling my girlfriend. I wrapped them in aluminum foil and thick plastic. I went to a park and buried them. With the remaining eight thousand, I told Carmen we would get married. In those days, I needed perfumes, and a friend of mine sold them. I went to see him at his house.

"Good afternoon, ma'am," I said to his wife. "Is Santos around? Because I came to buy some perfumes."

"Don't you know he was run over and is in the hospital?" she told me sadly.

"No! I didn't know," I replied surprised. "When did that happen?"

"A month ago, but he's better now," she told me. "He has casts on both legs and stomach. Here’s the address for you to visit him."

I went to see him at the hospital, and he was glad to see me.

Carmen Rosa and I went at the beginning of December to get the permit to get married, and we set the date for the sixteenth of that same month for our commitment.

On the fifteenth, we went to see Santos, who was already at home. It was around three in the afternoon. I got out of the car, and my fiancée stayed waiting for me. I chatted for a while with my friend and after buying him some perfumes, I said goodbye to him.

"Look, Santos," I said. "I’m leaving because I have to get ready for tomorrow. You see, I'm getting married."

"Great! If you have a little party, invite me, okay?" he said, joking.

"Well, I'm leaving because my fiancée is waiting for me in the car," I walked to the door and opened it. "There was the police parked in front of his house."

"What is the police doing parked there?" he asked doubtfully.

"I don't know," I replied with disinterest.

"Are you free of sins?" he said, looking at me with a mischievous look.

"Of course I am. Why do you ask that?" I said very seriously.

"Because it’s the first time I see the police parked here in front of my house. I don't know whose day they want to ruin."

16
A CRUEL CONFINEMENT

Santos and I kept talking without caring about the police officers.

"Well, Santos, I'm leaving," I said goodbye and headed to the car where my fiancée was. Carmen Rosa saw me and got out of the car, walking toward me. Suddenly, I heard a voice behind me.

"Hey! Hey! Hey you!" yelled the voice.

I stopped and turned around. I saw the police officers outside the patrol car with a piece of paper in hand.

"Are you calling me?" I said with a look of astonishment.

"Yes, you," they replied. I approached them.

"Are you Rolando Castillo?" they asked me.

"Yes, that's my name," I told them and remained thoughtful.

"We have to arrest you," they said and immediately took my hands to put the handcuffs on.

"What did I do to be arrested?" I asked the officer.

"I can't tell you why, I'm just following orders," the officer responded.

"I haven't done anything to be arrested," I told them in desperation.

"If you haven't done anything, why do you have an arrest warrant? Now avoid more trouble," the officer showed me the warrant.

I saw that it was true that I had an arrest warrant. On the sheet, I never read what the reason was.

My fiancée was screaming desperately and stood in front of me.

"No! Why do you want to take him?! If he hasn't done anything!" she screamed and wanted to hit them. "I'm sure it was that woman! She doesn't leave us alone!" she cried with tremendous desperation.

"Let me give this box of perfumes to my fiancée," I told the police officers.

"Okay, but hurry up because there's no time," they told me. From afar, Santos watched the scene and yelled at Carmen to leave the police alone, because they could also take her away.

"Look, miss, please step away, otherwise we'll have to arrest you too," a police officer told her and took her by the arm to move her away.

They took me to the police station and immediately took photographs of me in three positions and my fingerprints.

"Officer, why am I detained?" I asked the police officer who was taking the photos.

"I don't know, I'm just following orders," he replied.

I was very angry not to know why I was detained. To all the guards I asked, they told me the same thing: "just following orders".

They finished taking my fingerprints and took me to the same cell as last time. So I prepared so the mice wouldn't take my food this time. After three days, a guard came to see me.

"Rolando Castillo!" he shouted very loudly. "Hey, boy, get up because we're going to transfer you to the state prison!"

"But... why am I detained?" I asked the guard and not getting a response, I asked the same question again.

"I don't know," he said. "Just following orders."

"I think I have the right to know why I'm here," I told him desperately.

Another guard came and handcuffed me, pushing me against the wall and tightening the cuffs.

He looked at me with a lot of anger, while the other seemed to want to help me.

"I'll go get the permit for your transfer," the guard who had handcuffed me said.

As I felt pain in my hands, I called the other guard and showed him my hands.

"What happened to your hands, boy?" he said with surprise. "It's that the other police officer put the handcuffs on too tight, and my blood isn't circulating well," I told him. "I feel like my hands are getting numb."

"Well, I'll trust you," he replied. "Turn around, and I'll loosen the cuffs." He loosened them a bit. "Better now? Can you feel them?"

"Yes, thank you. At least you have a heart, and you realize that not all of us are the same," I told him, and he just nodded.

They put me in a police van. In twenty minutes we were at the state prison. One of the policemen who was taking me spoke on a radio and that big, heavy door opened.

When I saw that prison from the outside, it seemed very cold to me. And once inside, it immediately smelled of criminality. They got me out of the car and opened another big door and I entered another world. Unfortunately, I got a guard who was provocatively speaking to me from the moment I entered.

"And why are you here?" he would say with an angry face. "What did you do? Answer!"

"I don't know yet," I told him.

"Another one who didn't do anything! Look, be careful here," he said while taking my fingerprints. "Because I can control you, and I can do whatever I want with you. If I want to, I'll kill you! You are worth nothing! Just like all the ones here, who are just garbage!"

He treated me as if I were a dangerous criminal sentenced to death for being a rapist or robber. I had patience because I did not want those abusive men to beat me up.

When they finished doing all the paperwork, they sent me to take off my clothes and sprayed me with water from a hose. Then they bathed me with cold water, and the hose sprayed like the ones firefighters use to put out fires. The officer who had been provoking me before was the one who bathed me.

It was the first time I was in a state prison. I was astonished by what they were doing to me. I came to think they wanted to drown me because they aimed the water at my face to put it under the stream.

"Hey, leave me alone!" I shouted at them, and they ignored me. Through the stream of water, I managed to see how the two police officers laughed heartily, as if what they were doing to me was funny.

After abusing me in that way, they gave me four small soaps, a towel, a small toothpaste, a toothbrush, two white briefs, and the uniform that prisoners wear. I had to share the cell with a Puerto Rican who had been there for a while. When that guy saw me, he treated me very well. We became friends, and only three days later did I find out his name was Heriberto, but he was known as the "Chino."

The first nights I couldn't fall asleep. I spent the night thinking why I was there, what the real reason was. "It's not possible that woman did this to me. But I am sure she wasn't alone; someone else must be involved. But who? I feel so bad! I think I've been a danger to society. At least they should tell me. That way, I'd be more at peace! And if this was because of Lorena's lies, I think they should investigate the truth. How can it be possible that after everything she did to me, now I have to pay with this, something I don't owe? I'm here without knowing the cause and when I was about to get married. I was willing to change my life and start over.

"Cuba, why haven't you slept all these nights?" the "Chino" asked me. "What's got you so thoughtful?"

"It's just that I'm here locked up and I don't know the reasons," I told him worriedly.

"How did they imprison you without any reason in this place?" he said, amazed and looking at me intently.

"Yes, it's true," I told him.

"I can't believe it," he replied incredulously. "They put you here for some reason."

"Yes, if you don't believe me, give it time and you'll see. I'm not lying to you."

"Well, your case is strange," he replied. "Because at least I know I'm imprisoned for selling drugs. But your case is hard to believe. Look, Cuba, you need to sleep and not worry so much. In this place, one knows when they arrive, but not if they'll leave. Because many here get killed and that's the end of life."

"Who kills them?" I asked curiously.

"Sometimes the guards, by beating," he told me a little sadly. "Or sometimes the inmates themselves. You know, because of money or drug problems, or who knows what."

He fell silent, and I lay down on the bed. I started to sleep. I woke up when I heard someone banging on the bars.

"Let's go, let's go, it's lunchtime!" shouted the guard loudly who had bathed me when I arrived at that place.

"Hey, do the guards yell like that to tell us it's lunchtime?" I asked the "Chino."

"It's true, have you never been imprisoned before?" he asked.

"No, really," I replied desperately because he didn't believe me.

"Look, don't pay attention to the guard who just made that fuss. Don't even look at him because he's the worst and toughest in the prison. They call him the 'Scorpion'."

The "Chino" told all his friends that I was imprisoned without knowing the reason. And every five minutes they would ask me: "Cuba, is it true you're here without knowing why?" I was tired of hearing the same thing all the time.

Three months after being there, one day I decided to stay in my cell to write a letter to my children. I heard footsteps and saw it was the guard they called the "Scorpion."

"Why didn't you go out to the yard?" the guard asked me, standing in front of my cell bars.

I pretended not to hear him and continued lying on the bed writing. He kept insisting, in a provocative manner.

"I'm talking to you. Why didn't you go out to the yard with the other inmates?"

Since I didn't answer him, he had the bars opened and came in. I remained on the bed. Suddenly he took me by the feet and pulled me, throwing me to the floor.

"What do you want with me?" I said very seriously. "Because I see you want to get me into trouble and I'm not up for that."

He didn't like that I spoke to him like that and then he looked at the wall and saw some pictures hanging there. Among them was one of Jesus Christ, and then he said: "You can't have this here!"

"But what's wrong with you, sir?" I said, astonished at his attitude.

"Did you call me sir?" he said with a mocking smile. "Then how do you want me to call you? Because you're the one looking for trouble with me. I don't see anything wrong with calling you that. What I want is to avoid problems because I want to get out of here."

Since I didn't keep quiet and answered him, he got angrier and started throwing the pictures. At that moment the boys from the yard were coming and ahead of them was a guard.

"What's going on here, with this boy, officer?" the guard asked the "scorpion".

"Nothing has happened," the "scorpion" answered. "But in a few seconds something will happen with this stupid Cuban, for pretending to be religious."

The other guard started laughing and continued walking.

"Call me if things get complicated," he shouted, laughing. As I heard what they were saying, I ignored the guard again. At that moment the "Chino" came in.

"Cuba! What's happening between the guard and you?" he asked me scared.

"He's taking down the pictures because he feels like it. He wants to create problems for me and I'm not up for that."

The "Chino" approached the guard to tell him that the pictures were his and not mine, but the guard was so angry he pushed him with all his strength and threw him on top of me.

I got so angry that I was blinded, getting up from where I was and the guard and I started fighting. We threw punches down the hallway until we got near a staircase that led to the basement. I wanted to stop there, but the guard kept hitting me. I had no choice but to throw him down the stairs, falling to the bottom.

The other guards noticed and came running. They immediately handcuffed me. They took me to a very dark cell, separate from the others. I stayed there for four days, after which two guards came for me to take me to the Institution's Director.

"I had you brought here because you sent a man to the hospital. And I want to know how it happened and why," he asked me pompously.

"Sir, but first tell me why I'm here," I asked him, realizing he was the director. At that moment I felt hope and even forgot his question.

When the director saw that I didn't answer, he got angry and shouted with all his strength: "I asked you a question, stupid!"

I didn't know what to say. Then he called the guards.

"Take this stupid to the hole," he ordered them.

Since the director didn't say how long I would be there, I stayed there for nine months. But I didn't care anymore because I couldn't be more imprisoned. The "hole" was a small room with a very low voltage bulb, it didn't illuminate anything and you could only see that it was on from the pale orange color it emitted.

The only one I saw was a rat that always visited me, and I even saved food for it and gave it to it myself. Three months after being locked up there, the rat had eight baby rats, and since I didn't see or talk to anyone, I tried to pass the time with something. So I wanted to raise the little animals. When I had already prepared a small place for them, the sea took them one by one. I talked to the rat and it became my friend. That's how it began to come daily.

One day a priest came to see me and from then on he started visiting me every eight days. He helped me a lot because he intervened so I could be released from that prison.

I remember that day they gave me my civilian clothes. I was happily walking towards the exit, and my steps were giant; I felt I would never pass through that huge door. Near the entrance, I saw two guards dressed in green, different from those inside. They approached me.

"Hey, boy! What's your name?" they asked me.

I was thinking about what I would do. "Maybe I'll immediately get a job and start a new life again."

"Hey! Tell us your name," they asked me again.

"Oh... my name is Rolando Castillo," I replied fearfully. As soon as I told them my name, they put the handcuffs on me. They said they were from Immigration Police. And they took me to a white car parked outside that prison.

"But... why are you taking me?" I told them with terrible desperation. "What did I do now?"

They turned to look at each other and started laughing.

"That's something we don't know," they replied mockingly. "Because we don't decide anything."

I had no choice but to shut my mouth and follow their orders as they said. I remained silent while they drove. We arrived at a town called York, from there they took me directly to a maximum-security penitentiary.

"Here you will stay until other officers come to look for you. They will decide your case," that's all they told me and left.

"But what is my problem? What charges are there against me?" I shouted at them as they walked away.

I received no response. Another officer approached and gave me an orange uniform, like all the prisoners.

"Put on this uniform to take you inside."

I was really worried because I didn't know what was happening to me. I didn't know where they would transfer me next either. "Now I remember, John is Lorena's sister's boyfriend, and he was studying to be a lawyer. He is Cuban, and from the little we talked, he seemed like a nice person. Maybe he can help me. I'll try to find out how to reach him."

My desperation was such that I needed help from whoever, it didn't matter if it was family or someone related to that woman who got me into trouble.

Luckily, one of Lorena's sisters sent me a letter those days. In that letter, she said she wanted the keys to my car because I had left it parked in front of her house and before the police took it away, she planned to sell it and send me the money from it. I took advantage of the address she put in the letter and wrote to her sister who was the lawyer's girlfriend.

In five days, I received the response: "Dear brother-in-law, I'm already living with John. I mentioned your situation to him and he said he would request permission from the lawyers' commission to visit you. He is going to talk to you. Greetings from your kids. Love, your sister-in-law Laura."

After two weeks, a guard came to see me in my cell.

"Hey, Rolando Castillo, you have a visitor," he opened the gate to put the handcuffs on me. "Follow me!"

I was pleased to know someone was visiting me. I didn't know who it could be. I entered the visiting room. There John and another lawyer were waiting for me. I felt happy.

"How are you, John?" I greeted him very optimistically.

"Rolando, do you have the title of the car you left parked in front of Laura's house?" he said without greeting me.

"But... you haven't even asked me about my problem!" I replied upset. "And now you're talking about the car parked at your sister-in-law's house. Look, if that's why you came, you'd better go because I have nothing to give you."

He looked at me and laughed. I got even angrier.

"If all you're interested in is the car," I told him. "I'd better leave right now."

"No! Wait a little! With the car title, we can sell it, and with that money, you can pay for a lawyer," he said trying to convince me. "That way, you'll get out of here soon."

I was very angry and didn't want to listen to him. I left there.

"How is it possible that it comes to this? If he really wanted to help me, he wouldn't charge me anything. And when I get out, I'll pay him somehow. But with this, I don't want to hear anything more about that damn family."

I continued my usual routine in that place. I got it deep in my mind that I was alone in this country. I resigned myself to waiting for the day they would come to transfer me elsewhere. I spent almost four months in that place. Gradually, I adapted to the system and started making friends.

In those days, some guards arrived with papers in their hands. They started calling a few, and I was among them. They handcuffed us by the hands and feet and transferred us to Philadelphia. There we were put in a small cell. There were twenty of us, and we were very cramped and unable to bathe. We stayed three days in that little place, after which two police officers came alone for me and took me to the airport. I didn't know why. Just like before, now I was just as or more confused. I no longer asked why they did this to me. They took me to Atlanta. There, two guards were waiting for me.

"With this Cuban, you won't have any problems," the guards who brought me told those waiting for me. "Once he got aggressive, so don't trust him."

The guards took the plane back, and we made our way to the penitentiary.

"So you're very dangerous and a good fighter," the guards said as we were on our way.

"Yes, if you are going to take me to prison, then do it," I replied with a smile. "Because I'm not here to listen to nonsense."

"Look! Now I really think this little Cuban is very brave," they said. "But if you try to do something outside of what is allowed by our rules, you'll see that things won't go well for you. And now we'll take you to where the real bad guys are."

I knew they were provoking me, and I decided to ignore them. I remained silent the entire way. I don't know what hell is like, but when I arrived at that prison, I thought that was it. Inside, the smell of death was palpable. "Those policemen told me the truth. Here are the worst criminals. Why would they bring me here? But I'm prepared for whatever comes. Where are the policemen? They just left me and went away."

"Listen, kid, I'm going to take you to the cell blocks," said a guard who was there.

In the cell blocks, there were four more Cubans. One of them was not bad looking. Three African Americans, upon seeing him, started to harass him.

"Hey! Wait until they take you to the bathroom, and you're going to belong to us!" they shouted loudly. The Cuban was already scared.

I only thought about the time when they would take us to bathe.

"Guys! How about we unite the five of us, and as soon as they send us to bathe, we jump on the black guys?" said one of us. "We can't let these brutes come at us."

"Yes, you're right," said another guy. "We shouldn't allow them to abuse us. Not even from Castro did we back down, let alone these 'jerks'. "

That night I was thinking about how it would go the next morning because the black guys were still harassing a lot. However, the next day they didn't take us to bathe, allegedly because we were just passing through.

"Look, buddy," I said to the guy who had been harassed by the black guys. "In any prison, never trust any of these black guys, because they never forget anyone and sooner or later they catch you and do whatever they want with you."

I gave him that advice thanks to the little experience I gained in the prisons I set foot in.

I learned that in that prison there were many inmates who had arrived from Mariel in the same year as me, in 1980, and still hadn't seen the outside.

"Look, we have to hold a meeting to get us out of here or send us back to our country," I heard an older Cuban saying. "Because we are tired of being imprisoned."

I never learned about the plan they had. However, I agreed with them because I was going through a similar situation. It was not possible for them to deprive us of our freedom without knowing the reasons.

It was five in the morning when some guards came for me.

"You're ready, kid, because we're going to transfer you out of here."

"Where to?" I asked the guards, hoping they would tell me the next place.

"We don't know yet. Do you want to take a shower? There is still time."

I felt happy when they said that because I hadn't touched water since I left York. As soon as I finished showering and tidying up a bit, they put cuffs on me and took me to a truck that was already full of prisoners. I never knew where the place was, I only know they were some dungeons. Everyone with me that day was a real criminal. They treated me like them, even though I hadn't done anything.

For a long time, I thought Immigration people had confused me with my uncle because of the surname. "Maybe when they find out that I'm not the one they are looking for, they will then let me go free." But time stretched on and I became more desperate each day. They kept moving me from one place to another, serving a sentence that wasn't mine. "If I had stayed in Cuba, I wouldn't be going through this. And if for some reason I were in the same situation, at least I know I have my family and they would visit me. I also know I wouldn't worry so much about my future like here, where I don't know what I will do when I get out or how people will treat me."

In those days, I spoke with an officer who immediately seemed different from the others.

"Sir, tell me why they don't send me to my country. Being as I am, I would rather they send me back to my country even though I know they are going to kill me, but even that's fine."

"But we have nothing to do with Immigration laws, we just follow orders."

"But what are these Immigration laws? Why do they have non-criminal people locked up with those who are criminals and serving life sentences? Like in my case, I don't know why I'm here. However, I have to endure the anger and insolence of those murderers who are truly bad and treat us the same as them."

"I understand what you're trying to tell me," he said with a calm expression. "Maybe I can do something for you. But this has to stay between us."

"Really, can you help me?" I asked incredulously. "Tell me how," I said filled with joy.

"Look, I have a friend who works in Immigration, and I think he can do something for you. Give me a little time, and when I have a chance, I'll write him a letter. When I have a response, I'll send you a letter to Florida, which is where you'll be. I'm going to tell you something, but don't tell anyone."

"What is it?" I asked intrigued.

"I will accompany you to the Atlanta airport. And from there, they will take you to a newly built institution near a city called Tallahassee. The name of that institution is Mariana. I want you to give me your first and last name, and I will surely write to you soon. Don't despair, I will have something positive for you."

17
STARTING OVER

The next day, they transferred us to the airport. We were shackled hand and foot.

The truck arrived at the airport. There was a lot of federal security, maybe because of the high-risk prisoners who were with me or because of the Cubans who were there.

They boarded several prisoners onto a rather large plane. I never knew where they were taking them. I saw another plane landing. "I suppose they'll take us on that one. I hope they treat us better there than here." I snapped out of my thoughts when one of those at the end of the line suddenly started running towards the landing plane.

"Stop! Stop!" shouted a guard loudly.

The man kept running, handcuffed. The guard shouted at him again, and the man was like crazy. The police pointed a rifle at him and pulled the trigger. I saw how that man fell to the ground. Even wounded, he continued to crawl. Immediately, four more police officers arrived at where the prisoner was and began to beat him mercilessly.

"Don't hit him, you bullies!" we prisoners began to shout. "See, he's already wounded, and you still hit him!"

The police saw that we didn't like what they were doing and loaded the wounded man onto another truck. I don't know where they took him. Several prisoners were boarded onto the plane that had arrived.

"You will go directly to an institution called Mariana," explained the guard. "It is near the city of Tallahassee."

I don't know why, but when I arrived at that institution, I felt safer. Perhaps because the building was better. It looked like a school. There were many Cubans detained by Immigration. The guards weren't as harsh as those in other prisons. The place had a factory where they made office furniture and a varnish workshop. I met many Cubans who lived in my neighborhood in Cuba. They had been in this country for many years. They didn't know my family. There were also Mexicans, Guatemalans, Hondurans, Salvadorans, Chinese, Jamaicans, Colombians, etc.

A fellow I met told me that those who behaved well got out faster.

"Hey, why haven't you gotten out?" I asked the boy.

"Because I got into a fight here. You know, there's always someone looking for trouble, and if you let them, it's worse."

"And then they punished you with more years?" I asked incredulously.

"Yes, so be careful. Don't pay attention to provocations. Immigration comes every month and checks the files, and if there's someone who misbehaved, they definitely cut their freedom."

"I'm glad you told me. I'll try to avoid problems at all costs. Let's see if I can get out of here soon."

We were already at the end of 1990 when I saw my name added to a list to work cleaning the surroundings of the institution. I had to report early to a sergeant, who would tell us what job each of us would do. On Monday, I got up early and headed to the place where I was supposed to meet the sergeant. He put me to cut the grass. I was happy to do something. In the afternoon, I went for a walk in the yard with my roommate.

"Chao, you say you don't know my family, right?" I commented with dismay. "But you lived in the same neighborhood as me."

"Yes... yes, boy, a long time ago. I came to this country a long time ago. Is everything still the same there?" he asked wistfully. "When you left, could people still fish in the river?"

"No! Not at all! They ordered big nets to be installed and built a dam which they turned into a hatchery. But with all that, we still stole the fish from them. You know that the government only gives a kilo of fish to each family according to the government booklet? Do you think with that my family would eat? No! Boy! With that, it's like nothing!"

"Look, Chao, I'm leaving because I want to take a walk around the yard and I'll be back. Sit and rest, I'll be right back."

I took two laps and when I returned, the old man was with eight more boys. One of them was in a wheelchair.

"Look, guys, this little black guy is from the neighborhood!" he said loudly to the others.

I felt more confident, but I preferred to watch them from a distance. "Well yes... you see, I had a great friend in Cuba," the boy in the wheelchair was talking to Chao. I couldn't see his face because his back was turned towards me. "I cherished him so much, and cherished is an understatement. I loved him dearly. So much so that one day, without asking my mom's permission, I went with him to fulfill his military service. It wasn't my time yet, but I didn't want to be separated from my great friend. I didn't last long because I missed my dear mother... You know when one is a child? It's difficult to be away from mom. I remember we stole a tractor and then some horses to escape from that place. When we lived in Havana, we would sometimes catch the cats that a neighbor had and pull their tails. At other times, we would throw them far because, according to what people said, they had seven lives. That little black boy was a true friend... I called him 'Paita'."

But... you know, I came here and never saw him again. When I heard what he said, I started to move closer little by little discreetly. Upon hearing the last words... 'I called him "Paita"...' I felt such a strong emotion that my heart raced. Then I tried to see his face.

"I know who he is! For sure! It must be him! But what if it's not! Carlitos didn't use a wheelchair! It's been so long since we last saw each other, since 1978... when I helped him escape from the army and that was a long time ago..."

"Hey! What's this 'Paita' you're talking about?" I said, looking him straight in the eyes. He had a beard and long hair, and at that moment, I didn't recognize him. He turned to look at me and was thoughtful for a few seconds.

"No! I can't believe it!" he said very cheerfully. "You're 'Paita', come on, lift the right side of your pants!"

I laughed and he insisted. I lifted my pants and when he saw my burnt leg, he said "lift the other side". I didn't do it.

"You're Carlitos, Aleida's son... I couldn't continue speaking because a lump formed in my throat."

"Yes, I am... your friend," he said, his voice choked with emotion. "I am... Carlitos..." He didn't say more and tears fell from his eyes. Since he couldn't walk, I approached and hugged him. At that moment, I felt like I had someone from my family. And I had a tremendous desire to live.

It was 1990, it was October, and Immigration arrived to give us the news that they were going to interview the people they had selected, and I was among those people.

"Carlitos! Do you know something?"

"No 'Paita', what's up?"

"They just told me that Immigration chose me for an interview!"

"Stay focused, Ronaldito! Because not all of us have that opportunity!"

In the interview, they asked me about my uncle, as we had the same last name. According to them, there was a mix-up and they hinted that because of that they would release me, as it was a mistake they had made.

Two months after the interview, they posted lists of the people who would be released, and my name did not appear. At that moment, I felt the world fall apart. I started to investigate. A friend who worked in the offices managed to get me a copy of a document signed by the Director of the Institution stating that I used drugs and had been caught with alcohol in my bloodstream, and that I was even intoxicated. My desperation led me to find a way to talk to the director, but he never gave me the opportunity. When I managed to see him in the yard, he wouldn't face me.

"Carlitos! Tell me... do you have a girlfriend?"

"I'm married and have a daughter. When they come to see me, I'll introduce them to you."

"Maybe I won't be allowed to go to the visiting room," I replied resignedly. "But you see, I know a Colombian who has a girlfriend and says that his girlfriend's sister is also imprisoned. And you know... he's going to introduce me to her! She is Mexican."

"How will he introduce her? If they don't let us near the fence that separates us from them!"

"Look, Carlitos, don't tell anyone! But it's through letters!"

"How through letters? You see how it is here! They don't let you do anything!"

"Well, they do it! They throw the letters and they pick them up!"

"How do they do that? We're separated by almost fifty meters!"

"Well, we put a stone inside the letters and throw them hard so that they reach them. They do the same!"

"Look, better wait, and I'll introduce you to a friend from Miami. One of these days I'll send a letter and she'll come!"

As he never did, I talked to the Colombian and then he introduced me to his sister-in-law. I wrote her letters and threw them; she felt happy.

I was falling in love with that girl, but I knew we would never come to anything. On one occasion, several friends of mine were joking with the women from that prison, and I stepped aside because I didn't want the guards to see me. I couldn't get in trouble because Immigration officers would come, and I was hoping they would give me my freedom.

"Hey! Come closer," I told the Colombian. "Look, come here. Do me a favor."

"What's up, Cuban? What favor do you want?"

"Throw this letter to my girlfriend."

The Colombian threw it, and then we went into the cells so they could do the routine check to see if we were all present. I was preparing to continue writing my love letters when two guards came and took me away.

"Rolando! You have to come with us! Look, they found this letter of yours near the railing of the women's prison, and you can't deny it because there's a photograph of you inside!"

I got to the holding cells and then saw a sergeant who had read my letters days before and liked how I wrote. That officer was the one who had to punish me.

"Look, kid, here the punishment is three weeks. I'm not going to punish you for that long; in exchange, I want you to write a letter to my girlfriend. When you get out, don't tell the other inmates the deal we made."

"All right, don't worry, I won't."

I got out of there three days later and decided to end my relationship with the girl from the other prison. I didn't want any problems since my freedom was what interested me most. If they caught me again, I would never get out. Besides, I didn't have much time to visit her since I dedicated my hours to writing love letters for the companions who requested them. They paid me five dollars per letter. That way, I had money to buy notebooks, pens, and stamps. I had already become a true romantic writer. Chao, the old man I shared a cell with, used to tell me: "The little black kid is in love again." But what could I do if no one wrote to me?

"Hey, little black kid," Chao said to me, "there's a magazine with phone numbers and addresses of women looking for a partner. Why don't you write to one? If you want, I can ask my wife to bring me the magazine next time."

"All right, Chao, let's see if it works."

I eagerly waited for that magazine, and two months later it arrived. I decided to write to a Colombian girl. She replied to me and coincidentally had a brother in the same prison. After knowing each other for a month, she decided to come and see me. I was happy, and the day of the visit arrived.

We entered the room and greeted each other as if we had known each other forever. In that room, there was a little studio used for photography by one of the mates. Sometimes they paid him twenty dollars, and he would take care of things while a prisoner had sexual relations with the visiting woman.

On that occasion, after being locked up for two long years, it was my turn. I happily left that room, and from that moment on, things started to get better each day.

Carlitos' sister visited me, and we took some photos with her mother so she could take them to mine and let her know I was okay. I decided to distance myself a bit from my Colombian friend. One day, while we were cleaning around the prison, he shouted at me.

"Rolando! Come here, I have to tell you something," he called.

"What's up, Aceré?"

"Nothing, my sister-in-law wanted to commit suicide."

"Why?" I asked, surprised.

"Because of the letter you sent her. She says it's no longer worth living. That she didn't do anything to you for you to leave her like that."

"Yeah, I know. But you know I'd rather not have problems. Look, I need to get out of here. I'm serving a sentence unnecessarily."

"Yes, that's true. I understand you."

It was August of 1991 when the immigration officers came with a list of people who would be interviewed. I was very happy because my name was on the list.

"How did it go? Did they tell you they would release you this year?" my companions asked.

"I'm not sure because they're very tricky. They usually release who they want."

In October, immigration returned to give the names of those who would be released. I was surprised to see my name on the list of the twenty-one chosen ones.

Then I told the Colombian girl not to visit me because I was going to be freed.

At the end of November, the immigration representatives arrived to gather those who would be released.

"You are going to a half-house we have in Chicago. There you will stay for at least six months until you adapt to society. We will provide you with food and new clothes when you arrive. We will give you training and help you find work. While you are in the program and work, we will save your money and every weekend we will give you twenty percent of what you earn. The rest will be given to you when you complete the program and find a sponsor to support you. Then you will be free. You will not be able to leave Chicago for a year, but after this, you will be released forever. But you must meet the requirements."

Once the immigration agents left, we all returned to our cells. We tried to avoid trouble, but the prison guards started provoking us. They knew we were leaving, so they started bothering us. Sometimes they would wake us up at three in the morning just to ask if we were sleeping well. Although we got angry, we couldn't respond badly. If we did, they could mess up our freedom just by reporting to the warden. And since it was their word against ours, the warden always believed them.

There was a boy who had diabetes and every day at three in the morning they would let him out to get his insulin. However, one night they locked the cell and didn't open it at his medicine time. He was found dead in the morning, and the guards pretended to know nothing. On other occasions, they would cut off the water when we were soaped up during bath time, laughing at us loudly.

Finally, the day of our release came and we packed our allowed belongings. I had to sell some sports suits, my sneakers, gold chains, etc., which they prohibited me from taking. I didn't know the reason.

They put chains on our hands, feet, and straps around the waist. We complained that they kept treating us like criminals when we were about to be free.

"If you don't shut up, you'll face the consequences," a guard yelled at us. "Now we are in charge and we can take away your right to be free."

We all shut up and then they took us to the airport. We boarded a plane that took us to Atlanta. When we arrived, we were treated very badly due to the recent Cuban uprising in prison. We were placed with the most troublesome people. I opted to be alone. As in the other prison, here I also dedicated myself to writing poems and love letters, keeping them for myself even though I had no one to send them to.

One day, some inmates fought and one of them stabbed the other in the neck. I saw the blood gush as if a faucet had been opened. The injured man tried to go down the stairs but only managed to descend a few steps before falling uncontrollably, leaving everything covered in blood.

The guards entered immediately, handing out blows to everyone in their path.

When I saw the guards coming, I went into my cell and lay down on the bed to avoid trouble. They closed the cells for us.

From comments, I learned that the injured man died before being taken out of there. We spent almost two months in that prison and then we were handcuffed again and taken to the airport. We boarded a plane bound for the federal prison in Texas.

The guards here were more military-like than elsewhere. They made us work cleaning the prison grounds. There were many activities like golf, soccer, tennis, basketball, etc. Sometimes people from outside would come to play baseball with the prison team. There was a very large gym, but like everywhere, there were many homosexuals with AIDS who bothered some in the showers. They didn't bother me, but others were victims of abuse.

I was worried to see how many people were taken away each week without us knowing anything about our freedom. After a few months, they put the chains on us again and put us on a truck that took us to Houston, Texas. It was a small prison and we spent the night without eating anything. The next day they took us to the airport.

We were all dirty and with a terrible smell of sweat. We boarded a plane and at the door, they took off our chains.

I remember my heart was pounding, I felt as if I was shedding a weight I had been carrying for a long time. I finally felt free. Once inside the plane, we were given a great breakfast, something I hadn't eaten in a long time. I asked for more food and they served us all double. For me, at that moment, my life was starting anew. I promised myself never to go back. I completed the year of work and in the end, I found a sponsor who helped me become completely free. Now I believe that nothing justifies depriving oneself of freedom with violence. Life in prison is too painful and cruel. I believe it's worth living to nurture the spirit. In my case, my situation was different, and it's difficult not to hold a grudge against those who did me so much harm without reason. However, we must be positive to have strength and rebuild our lives.

www.ingramcontent.com/pod-product-compliance
Lightning Source LLC
LaVergne TN
LVHW010542160826
845677LV00013B/2971

* 9 7 9 8 8 9 5 6 9 3 7 7 3 *